SPRING AND ALL

Other works by Red Wheelbarrow Writers:

This Uncommon Solitude: Pandemic Poetry from the Pacific Northwest
ISBN 978-1-7344945-4-9

So Much Depends Upon . . . : An Anthology
ISBN 978-0-9724960-3-2

Memory into Memoir: An Anthology
ISBN 978-0-9724960-5-6

Spring and All

An Anthology

Written and edited by
Red Wheelbarrow Writers

Sidekick Press
Bellingham, Washington

Published 2023
Printed in the United States of America
ISBN: 978-1-958808-12-2
LCCN: 2023935693

The original book, *Spring and All*, by William Carlos Williams, was published in 1923 and entered the public domain in 2019.

Sidekick Press
2950 Newmarket Street, Suite 101-329
Bellingham, Washington 98226
https://sidekickpress.com

CONTENTS

By the road to the contagious hospital
by William Carlos Williams
(1883-1963)

By the road to the contagious hospital
under the surge of the blue
mottled clouds driven from the
northeast-a cold wind. Beyond, the
waste of broad, muddy fields
brown with dried weeds, standing and fallen

patches of standing water
the scattering of tall trees

All along the road the reddish
purplish, forked, upstanding, twiggy
stuff of bushes and small trees
with dead, brown leaves under them
leafless vines—

Lifeless in appearance, sluggish
dazed spring approaches—

They enter the new world naked,
cold, uncertain of all
save that they enter. All about them
the cold, familiar wind—

Now the grass, tomorrow
the stiff curl of wildcarrot leaf
One by one objects are defined—
It quickens: clarity, outline of leaf

But now the stark dignity of
entrance—Still, the profound change
has come upon them: rooted, they
grip down and begin to awaken

Preface
by Linda Lambert

In 1923, one hundred years ago, William Carlos Williams' *Spring and All* was privately published in Paris: ninety-three pages of quirky experimentation—upside-down headings, a sprinkling of typographic irregularities, chapters purposely out of order, and untitled poems known only by their first lines. Despite its low initial print run of three hundred copies, *Spring and All* contained poems that endured, including "The Red Wheelbarrow," the inspiration for Red Wheelbarrow Writers, a loose affiliation of working writers who produce independently, and who join together to support, encourage, and sustain one another.

The editors' call for submissions for Red Wheelbarrow Writers' fourth anthology said William Carlos Williams was considered "an uplifting voice amid the harsh realities of the world." They cited the concluding lines of the first poem in the collection:

—Still the profound change
has come upon them: rooted, they
grip down and begin to awaken

Writers were invited to contribute unique, uplifting stories. Before writing my own uplifting story—and I didn't yet know what it might be—I felt driven to understand the optimism the editors attached to Williams, especially in reference to the quoted poem.

Like me, you may have wondered about the image of a contagious hospital as a springboard for hope. You might have read the first dozen lines and noticed negative images: mottled clouds, dried weeds, the waste of muddy fields, standing water, dead brown weeds, leafless vines, and the reddish, purplish, forked, upstanding, twiggy stuff of bushes, not to mention the thrice-used word "cold." Unwise as it may be to judge the theme of a poem by its first line, "contagious" suggests bleakness.

Reading poetry takes patience, and I am not always a patient reader, but I began to picture Williams, a medical doctor, absorbing the landscape near the hospital where he worked, not far from his home in Rutherford, New Jersey. At the fourteenth line of the "contagious" poem, a new season begins in slow motion: "lifeless in appearance, sluggish/dazed spring approaches." The previous dormant or distressed elements of nature "enter the new world naked." And then, "Now comes grass, tomorrow/the stiff curl of wildcarrot leaf."

At that last phrase, I fell in love with the poem. Out of what had seemed austere emerged curiosity and, yes, uplift. I had never heard of or looked at "the stiff curl of wildcarrot leaf," a beautiful description. The image of wild carrots and their leaves led me to a series of definitions that read like poetry: herbaceous biennial, roseate, hairy-stemmed, leaves—feathery and lacy, pinnately divided. At the end of the poem, Williams captured and signaled spring's beginning by the appearance of roots: "they/grip down and begin to awaken."

A close reading of "By the road to the contagious hospital" convinced me that Williams was an optimist, especially considering that he was writing in the aftermath of World War I. We are living in the aftermath of COVID and in the middle of political divisiveness, perhaps seeking a metaphorical spring.

The editors wanted "stories . . . to lighten our spirit." So I turned from "By the road to the contagious hospital," to search for lighter information about William Carlos Williams. At Western Washington University's Wilson Library, instead of academic titles like Terrence Diggory's *William Carlos Williams and the Ethics of Painting* or Bram Dijkstra's *Cubism, Stieglitz, and the Early Poetry of William Carlos Williams*, I selected a thin paperback: *I Wanted to Write a Poem*, published in 1958. Williams was listed as the author, but the title page bore an additional credit: "Reported and edited by Edith Heal."

In the mid-1950s, Ms. Heal was a student at Columbia University. She had the enviable experience of sitting with the poet and his wife at their home in New Jersey. Williams pulled publications from his bookcase and talked about each one, including *Spring and All*, which he called "a mixture of philosophy and nonsense." He said that "By the road to the contagious hospital" was "praised by the conventional boys for its form." I didn't know who the "conventional boys" were—critics?—and Ms. Heal didn't ask, but her book was packed with incidental asides and arresting anecdotes. I didn't have time to check it out, so I placed it on the shelving cart as instructed, planning to return the next day. But the next day when I returned to grab it, *I Wanted to Write a Poem* wasn't there—not on the cart, not reshelved. The volume had vanished into some kind of library thin air.

A week later, a friend took me to a bookstore she liked: Sideshow Books on La Cienega in Los Angeles. We entered a store crowded with teetering stacks of overflow volumes and a motley assortment of mismatched bookshelves. A middle-aged man with a California tan emerged and introducing himself as Tony, the owner. He offered espresso and gave us a chatty orientation about the categories of his "second-time around" material—from Hollywood posters to aviation stories, historical novels to art books. Tony said he was unable to resist buying books wherever he found them: thrift stores, estate sales, friends who were moving. Eventually, he had to open a bookstore to house them. Prices penciled on the title pages were "only guidelines, so make me an offer."

"Do you have any books by William Carlos Williams?" I asked.

"Check out the poetry section." He smiled, and waved us to an area about ten feet away.

The poetry section had only one book by William Carlos Williams: a good used copy of *I Wanted to Write a Poem*. The penciled price: $11. I had to have it, but I didn't want to pay more than its cover price, $8.95. Would he take $7.50?

"Sure!" he said. Then I told him about the book's disappearance from the library collection.

"The book found you," Tony said. "It happens all the time around here."

And now, this anthology has found you. Red Wheelbarrow Writers' *Spring and All* contains a variety of poetry, fiction, and nonfiction, wedded together by a common theme: uplift. Having endured several weighty years, the editors hope these stories and poems will help lighten the spirit as we seek a literary and metaphorical spring, observing "the stark dignity of entrance" and "the profound change" as the natural world, "rooted . . . grip[s] down and begins to awaken."

In the Hardy Zone
by Drue BeDo

Isolation. Buried deep in the dark, dank soil with my pointy end up, I have these past few years felt like a corm of crocus. Not to be confused with a cornucopia, a kernel of corn, or a kennel of corn dogs—a crocus corm is one of the earliest awakening bulbs awaiting the alarm clock of spring. A tight little fist of unfurled flower. Inside the corm, a colorful, petaled promise of hope sleeps until ready.

I am that tight fist.

I am so ready to bloom.

Hibernation. Apparently, my cluster of corms and I need to be planted in the hardy zone to experience a period of cold weather in order to flourish. Check. Last winter, I survived record freezing temperatures in the Pacific Northwest, sans furnace. Scraping a snow cone's amount of frost from the inside of each of my bedroom windows with a Hopkins Subzero ice scraper I'd excavated from the trunk of my car, I sang a sultry "It's cold *inside*," and sent it as a little Christmas video to friends gathered around their warm and toasty hearths. Friends who had obviously forgotten I live alone. I could have died. Honestly. Days upon days of carbon monoxide belching from my defunct, thirty-year-old furnace landed me in the emergency room suffering symptoms of dizziness and shortness of breath. I thought these were just symptoms of what happens to extroverts over fifty-five with long-term exposure to isolation and acute loneliness, but the nurse assured me, "You've been poisoned." So, I returned home and turned off the thermal beast and pretended I was back in Kathmandu where most people survive winters without central heating, heaping onto their beds mountains of blankets under which entire families pile to sleep after the warmth of the sun disappears. November, December, and January, I shuffled around in my yellow down sleeping bag—unzipped at the ankles for my feet to poke through, snugged tightly around my face to keep my head warm. I imagined myself a giant banana slug as I brewed hot coffee, plugged and unplugged space heaters, and listened to NPR announcers grimly forecast weeks upon weeks of more sub-degree temperatures. Flourishing seemed a distant dream.

Devastation. Gardeners state that corms are supposed to be "planted in groups and clusters" instead of being "spaced as individuals along a sidewalk." Botanists suggest that we live best with only a few inches between us. "Single flowers," it's been written, "get lost in the landscape." Perhaps city planners used such reasoning to validate their rezoning of single-family neighborhoods under the pretense of sprouting affordable housing. Ha! We corms whisper in the dark, our ears are underground. We know perfectly well that greedy developers invade like renegade weeds not to "cluster," but rather to "clusterf#*k" entire local landscapes with their multimillion-dollar, boundary-overlapping, multi-family monstrosities! As the bulldozers rage, let me be the deviant corm. Plant my point next to nothing but a wise old tree in a remote field, please. Bury me deep where the sidewalk ends!

Inebriation. "Prone to rot and mold if kept too moist." Corms and humans have so much in common. Notice the beautiful collection of colorful bottles in various shapes and sizes so many of us accrued during the pandemic, and by which we kept ourselves maybe a bit too moist. Perhaps I should have extracted myself from rot, mold, and fermentation, but, alas, looking out my back door and kitchen window upon not one but two greedy developers' multiplex manifestations of devastation, inebriation soon led to severe hibernation. (See how my little "ations" all cluster together so nicely—just inches from one another?)

Waiting for something to break open, boil, or burst forth is oftentimes exhausting. I came to wonder if these years of isolation, hibernation, devastation, and inebriation might miraculously result in a blooming, spiritual renovation. Did I have enough faith in my pink petals ever emerging again? And, if they did, were they truly hardy enough to withstand any additional Arctic winds life might blast in my direction?

In the language of flowers, crocus means cheerfulness.

I am trying.

Transformation. Now that spring is coaxing me to push my pointy parts up out of the cold, hard ground, I am daring to be hopeful. The lack of furnace in the dead of winter didn't freeze me. I embraced the cold. I now swim, year-round (despite rain, snow, and wind) in the exhilaratingly cold waters of the Salish Sea wearing just my mittens, stocking cap, and skivvies. Bitter loneliness didn't defeat me. I've begun inviting strangers, tired of sitting alone staring at their laptop screens in cafés, or other shoppers mumbling about the high price of kale at local grocery stores, to come share in lively conversational potlucks around my dining table once a month. Years of searching for meaningful employment as a theatre artist in a town besotted with coffee shops and brewpubs hasn't completely sunk my spirit. I am engaged in a 180-degree pivot and have struck up delightful international correspondences with theatre artists in Stockholm, Auckland, Munich, and Oahu. The loss of three dear friends has made me cherish my true and blessed companions who actively and reciprocally share a deep and loving connection—reading stories aloud to one another over the phone, hiking together up to alpine lakes and through old growth forests, inventing new recipes and dancing in one another's kitchens.

My small fist is ready to flower into fingers of future fortune and frolicking. I am summoning the worms as foot-soldiers (ignoring that they are, of course, pacifists and have no feet), rallying the ladybugs as beacons to light my way up and out of this darkness into glorious sunshine. Let the mice and moles dare to chew me up or pull me under, I am casting off this frozen-solid soil and reaching skyward. Watch me unfurl, hail or high water. Note my strength and fortitude. Rejoice as this mighty little crocus corm explodes in a revival of color and delight—so much more than a mere spring fling—this is a Spring Awakening of Hallelujah! Amazing grace! It's about time! And, of course, Thank the Blessed Holy Mother Earth!

Spring
by Carla Shafer

The doyenne,
essence of four
seasons undefeated—
seed packets and catalogs
never far from reach.

She comes
to the window,
raises the blinds,
peers into the yard
damp and eager to bloom.

Sentience fuses
to rain waters as it
permeates soil. Emergent
branch buds and crocus
leaves surge.

Her pulse—persistent
from season to season—
until harvest when
the edible fragrance
of spring caresses your hand.

Climbing Half Dome
by Lora Hein

When I started work as a maid in Yosemite Valley I had pinch-myself moments every day. Emerging from a hotel room, bleach bucket in one yellow-gloved hand, sponge in the other, my eyes would be drawn up through gaps in the adjacent screen of ponderosa pines and cedars. Frazil ice fanned out on either side of Yosemite Falls. Golden light from the sun's weak warmth sparkled on frozen chunks as they broke apart and drifted down.

Every midwinter day, I would trod the path from the girls' employee dorm to the Yosemite Lodge cafeteria, awestruck by gaps in the mist. Those low-hanging clouds obscured lower layers of the three-thousand foot cliffs and monoliths, revealing a slice of the rim with pencil points of conifers draped in fresh snow, brightened by first light. By lunchtime, remaining wisps would frame cliffs streaked with dark drizzles where water had run off, providing moisture for granite-clinging lichens and mosses to create abstract arrangements.

Art and drawing classes throughout high school and my first year of college failed me in imagining how I could render what I saw into anything as riveting as the constant changes in the scenery. After dropping out following my first year at Mills College, I made an impulsive decision the following fall to escape my evening custodial job at a burger joint in Oakland and flee to the cleaner air of Yosemite. The contrast from city cacophony to the stillness of that deep valley provided the space I needed to sort out my next steps.

As spring came, bringing the slanting sun rays deeper into the valley more hours each day, I spent my days off exploring the edges of the valley floor. Anywhere I could get closer to the confining rock cliffs drew me to run my hands over the speckled bases of those towering walls, intrigued with the variations I found. Leaning back, I became obsessed with wanting to explore beyond the limits of what I could examine close up.

A summer camp helper position released me from the restrictive crowding of the valley into the higher elevation meadows surrounded by spires that had stood above the glaciers that carved out the valley.

That fall, after the crowds of visitors thinned, I returned to my Yosemite Lodge job. The north-facing cliffs became a dark backdrop to branches of black oaks dappled with light-shimmering, golden leaves slicing through the opening at the west end of the valley. My yen to explore the confines of what I could get to pulled me towards enrolling in a class at the Yosemite Mountaineering School. It had been established the previous year, in 1969.

At my first and only class, I learned how to wrap inch-wide tubular webbing around my waist and in a figure eight to support each of my legs. I also learned to tie a bowline knot in the hemp rope that would protect me from harm if I fell. A carabiner, an oval of metal with a hinged clasp, clipped the loop of the rope to my webbing harness.

The instructor, Lloyd Price, gathered our small class at the base of a slanting rock at the toe of what appeared from the ground to be a towering cliff face. This seven-hundred-foot high buttress was tucked in the trees away from the road, between and out of view from its giant neighbors, El Capitan and the Three Brothers.

First Lloyd instructed us in the intricacies of knots and harnesses. Then he demonstrated the basics of belaying. We took turns, still safely on the ground, fastening ropes to each other, gripping the free end in one hand while letting the line attached to our partner slide through the other. We wrapped the static hand around our hips and across our bellies to bring enough friction to the line to keep the end attached to our partner from playing out.

When we had demonstrated our new skill to the teacher's satisfaction, his assistant climbed the rock, showing us different techniques to use our hands and feet to move upward. We could choose to stay on the smooth face of the granite, which, on closer inspection exhibited small bumps, narrow ridges, and broken flake edges on which to place the side of a boot sole or fingers or the palm of our hands. The other option was a vertical crack separating one side of the slab from a protruding rock. The opening was wide enough to jam in fingers, toes, or an entire hand.

"Always keep three points of contact with the rock, both hands and one foot or both feet and one hand, when moving the opposite hand or foot," Lloyd reminded us.

When the assistant had secured himself on a ledge above us, his feet dangling over the edge, it was our turn.

One by one we watched our classmates before making our own way up the rock, encouraged and guided by the instructor.

"Push your hips away from the temptation to hug the rock. When you stick your butts out, you increase the friction that keeps you on the rock."

While I waited, I pressed one palm against the rough granules of the granite. The embedded crystals varied in size, shape, and color. Many were no larger than a fingernail or toenail clipping, varying from slender, rectangular, black hornblende to shiny, flat chips of mica, milky squares of feldspar, and glassy filler of quartz crystals.

My mind was a jumble, trying to remember all the instructions when my turn came. Once I had made half-a-dozen placements of hands and feet, encouraged with suggestions and "That's the way!" from the ground, everything around me faded from focus. I zoned in on the texture of the rock, the feeling of my hands wedged against the rough surface inside the crack, and the irregularities found with each exploration of foot or fingers.

All at once, the rope ahead of me bent over the rounded ledge and I was hoisting myself onto the flat surface. I turned, sat, and clipped the loop of webbing fastened to an anchor point into the carabiner attached to my sit harness.

"Off belay," I announced.

The climber who had been belaying me responded, "Belay off."

At his signal I unclipped the rope and moved over on the ledge to make room for the next climber. Looking beside me, I wondered if the grin on my face was as broad as those on my fellow students.

The final exciting experience of the day was learning to rappel. To be extra secure, we not only held the rappel rope looped through the carabiner on our harness in one hand against our thighs, but we were also belayed by a rope attached to the rock. One by one we stood at the tipping point where the ledge turned vertical.

"Lean back and keep leaning, face the sky," Lloyd urged each in turn.

My toes left the edge and my heels held to the cliff we had just ascended.

Parallel to the leaf-covered sand over one hundred feet below, I pushed my feet away from the solid surface and allowed my weight to be held by the rope. Then, one step at a time, at first, and then, as I gained confidence in the holding power of the rope's friction against my body, coupled with the rope being played out by the belayer, I pushed off and lightly bounced both feet at a time. Like a moon walker taking tentative and then giddier steps, I played with the pull of gravity against the grip of Vibram soles on granite, and bounded sideways down the cliff.

I could not recall ever feeling so elated. In that moment the territory available for exploration unfurled. Before, I could only gaze up. Now I could climb to places previously out of reach.

Over the course of the next two months, I found a couple of climbers camped in the Sunnyside campground across the road from Yosemite Lodge who had the skill, equipment, and willingness to take a novice along on easy practice climbs.

During the winter, with climbing at a pause, I saved money earned working as a clerk at the Lodge front desk to purchase a bright, neon-colored, state-of-the-art rope, sling material for a harness, and a few carabiners. As I could afford to, I added a piton hammer, a selection of pitons, and more sling material for my growing hardware rack.

When the weather warmed the following spring, I was away from the valley, having resumed college classes in my new interest, geology, where I was one of two females in the class. As soon as I got back to my job at the Lodge over summer vacation, I met another woman who, like me, preferred to avoid the sometimes proprietary attitude of some of the male climbers who were willing to take a "chick" on a climb, but not without an expectation of favors owed.

Anne Marie had been climbing all spring and even though her skill was greater than mine, she was willing to practice easier climbs with me. We were soon doing mid-level difficulty climbs together. Unlike me, Anne Marie wasn't holding down a job and had more time to devote to climbing. Her greater confidence put her in the lead on our climbs. She was full of ideas to stretch our competence.

We were an unlikely pair. Anne Marie had a tendency to strut, especially around the guys in Camp 4, thrusting her broad shoulders back to appear taller than her more typical female height, and showing off on the pull-up bar tied between two trees. Although I was a head taller than her, I shrank to avoid revealing my shyness as well as my lack of upper body strength—no matter how much I practiced, pull-ups were impossible. I made up for it with legs trained on the sixty-two steps I had run up and down between my childhood home and the street since age three.

Anne Marie prodded me to try difficult climbs. Her choices of routes often included chimneys, wide cracks between rocks that required wedging one's entire body into the space. I had no desire to enclose myself in those cramped interiors.

The constant presence of Half Dome loomed large at the head of the valley, turning the pink glow of her tear-stained cheek to us at the end of each day. At some point, Anne Marie floated the idea of climbing that imposing icon. There was a route up the rounded curve along the southwest side, the one that faced Glacier Point. It was called Snake Dike.

In my geology classes that spring I had learned a dike is a vein of rock that forms when the molten soup of minerals, still buried beneath the surface, has begun to solidify. The darker minerals—

hematite, apatite, and mica—cool sooner than the pale pink feld-spar and clear quartz.

Sometimes blocks of rock crack when they cool quickly. Liquid quartz and feldspar squeeze into the openings. There, small crystals form first and then larger chunks of individual minerals solidify. The process is similar to forming rock candy out of a solution of sugar and water. These crystals are very hard. When the larger rock is exposed by erosion of overlying layers, those larger crystals resist erosion more than adjacent, fine-grained rock.

When we viewed Half Dome from Glacier Point and the light-ing was just right, these dikes stood out in relief on the southwest flank like the veins on the back of my hand. Three ingenious climbers had pioneered a route following those vein lines. Where no cracks existed to insert hands or pitons, they had drilled holes and inserted bolts into which they clipped a carabiner. By string-ing a climbing rope between these clips, they secured protection for ascending the vertical portion that curved at the top of Half Dome.

The climb would be the longest and toughest challenge either Anne Marie or I had attempted. It was technically within our ability level. However, when word got out among the climbers camped in Sunnyside campground, they taunted us, "Some of us will stay in camp to rescue you girls when the exposure freaks you out."

We were determined to prove them wrong. In early September 1971, we hoisted our frame packs, laden with ropes, slings, and climbing shoes in addition to overnight gear, and hiked the trail past Vernal and Nevada Falls. Then we struck out cross-country, up the slope to the base of Half Dome, where we camped for the night. The next morning, while the sun was hidden by the rock, we stowed our backpacks near the base.

Anne Marie took the lead for the first, and most challenging, pitch. I followed, and once I surmounted that difficult step, I relaxed, knowing nothing ahead would be as demanding. When I reached her at the first pair of belay bolts, Anne Marie asked if I would like to lead the next one-hundred-fifty-foot stretch. Even though I had only led one pitch on a short climb a month before, I agreed. She played out the rope as I ascended an increasingly steeper section that brought me to the first bolt. I clipped a carabiner to it and slipped the rope into its oval. As I progressed upward, the rope, tied with a bowline knot to my harness, played out of Anne Marie's hands through the carabiner clipped to hers.

With each upward step, I became entranced. The dike was as wide as my body, and snaked up towards the clear blue sky. Crystals of every shape were clustered along its entire length in knobs and cubic projections bigger than my fist. Never more than a foot separated choices to pick for resting my feet or wrapping my hand. The dike felt like a sparkling ladder. With each step and handhold, my exhilaration grew.

Before I could wonder how much farther I had to go, the double bolts of the first belay anchor appeared. I clipped myself in and called down to Anne Marie, "Off belay."

Moments later she responded, "Climbing."

"Climb on."

I leaned against the smoother rock beside the dike, my heels braced on two enormous blocks of feldspar. When I looked down, I realized how sheer the drop was. I could see the tree at the base where we had left our packs, the trunk hidden beneath the upper branches. The rope dangled free of the rock as I reeled it in with each upward move Anne Marie made.

When Anne Marie joined me at the belay point, she said little for several seconds. Then, leaning towards the rock, she said, "I'm sorry, I can't take the next lead. I don't know if it's something I ate, but I am feeling nauseous and don't think I can do it."

"That's okay, I'm feeling fine and I can take the lead from here all the way."

"Are you sure?"

"Positive. As long as you're up to following."

She nodded.

And I did. I left Anne Marie at each belay point and scaled that causeway of magnificent crystals in bliss. I had never before or ever since felt euphoria as tremendous and encompassing as I did for the hours that transpired. The sun made its way around the shadowing dome and the crystals gleamed brighter in its glow. I was beaming as brilliantly as those rays striking and refracting through the facets of endlessly fascinating shapes I stepped upon, lifting myself up and up with each step and handhold.

Anne Marie spoke little the rest of the climb. When I asked how she was doing, she nodded. There were no words to express my joy, so I assumed she felt equally speechless.

Years later, Anne Marie confided that she thought I was crazy. She admitted her nausea was due to exposure. The entire time she was belaying me while I was leading the second pitch, she imagined what would happen if I slipped, bouncing past her before the rope caught on the bolt above. She feared the force of my accelerating fall would pop bolts like a zipper. Then she would be pulled with me to the bottom, hundreds of feet below. All the while I had been oblivious to peril in my ecstasy of certain success.

The slope became less steep as we reached the final anchor bolt. There we coiled the rope in silence. We followed the dwindling strips of more worn and paler gems that blended into the vast summit of the dome. My exhaustion from the lengthy ascent caught up with me as we toiled up the remaining slope. As it began to level off, Anne Marie pulled out her Polaroid camera and snapped a victory photo of me, grinning at our accomplishment.

As we crested the highest point, the expanse of the high country came into view. Arrayed on the far side of the immense rock obscuring our vista, the ridge of Clouds Rest spread its beckoning arm toward the peaks of the Sierra. The pyramid of distant Mount Conness and closer pinnacles glistened in the lowering light of the waning day. Below our exalted perch, the valley was a deep gash, shadowed by the tower we stood on. I looked down at the promontories of El Capitan, North Dome, and Glacier Point, each of their summits more than a thousand feet below where I stood.

I had ascended a stairway of fist-sized minerals to reach unfettered vistas in every direction. Gleaming facets of blocky feldspar and glittering hexagonal clumps of quartz, sparkling visions of all I had touched, permeated my mind's eye. I stretched against the weight of rope coiled on my shoulder to pull myself up to my full height, feeling as if I could step onto the gathering afternoon cumulus.

Beach
by Nadia Boulos

Glistening sand
Dunes under my feet
Stretching for miles
Footprints stamped
Disturbing particles
Tracing shallow paths

Waves rolling
With a soft cadence
Patient, unrushed
Begging for a listen
Slow down, they say
Slow down.

Tears touch lips
My soul craves a reunion
As the Salton Sea
craves a splash
My tears, a perpetuation
of ocean, not yet of earth.

The Morning Comet
by Edward Tiesse

The flare
caught
the corner of my eye.

I whirled my head
in the 4:00 a.m.
winter darkness
among the stars
it blazed.

Its ease
of discovery
surprised me.

Like a warm water ship
leaving a phosphorous wake
its fairy dust tail
splashed against
the blackness.

Its luminescence
hypnotized
me.

My feet numbed
my arms shivered
my ears ached
in the cold.

I watched.

Slowly it swam
across the sky
until
its tail faded into the
dark morning.

It was
like youth
so brazen
so confident
so unafraid
so short
lived.

Conifer Girl
by Edward Tiesse

When she can't sleep at night
she tiptoes around the foot of the bed.
Trying not to wake me,
she opens and closes the bedroom door.
If it's summer,
she goes outside to see
the moon and if any stars
are falling.
In the morning she tells me
there weren't any falling stars
but she did hear
a Barred owl.

When she can't sleep at night
she rises from our bed
and studies gardening books
as if she had a final exam
in the morning.
She's developed
an interest in conifers
and has had hours of conversations
at all the nearby nurseries

discussing which will best flourish
in full sun, partial shade, on the windy side
of the yard.
At one nursery her intense curiosity
has been noticed
and they nicknamed her
Conifer Girl.

The Diner
by Richard Little

The chrome railroad diner sat beside a forgotten north-south state highway on the outskirts of a small town. Gray-green pine woods ran to the east; yellow dry-grass hills disappeared in the west. The restaurant's patina had seen better days, but neon in the window announced "OPEN." Alec's tires crunched gravel and splashed through obligatory Northwest rain puddles as he pulled into the small parking lot. He shut the truck off and sat for a moment listening to the *tick, tick* of the quiet engine, then sighed and got out.

"Cindy's Kitchen" was the kind of place his dad chose on their road trips together, Dad on business, teenage Alec out of school for the summer: unpretentious with some cars parked in front. The dad whose unshaved stubble had scraped Alec's cheek while they hugged and cried together, until the nurse came in and suggested the still-young old man needed to get some sleep. He'd been just the other side of sixty, for Christ's sake!

Unpretentious or not, there are not many eateries in the U.S. where you can go in after wilderness camping for a week—no shower, just a dousing of creek water, rumpled camp shirt and stained khakis, hat-hair—and not risk being underdressed.

"Cindy's" looked like such a spot. Alec chose a stool, its vinyl seat less cracked than its neighbor, and brushed away a few crumbs before sitting down. He still had standards, after all. Behind the counter, a woman of indeterminate age came his way. She plopped down a glass of water and silverware and a packet of slightly crushed soda crackers, then handed Alec a laminated menu. A tangle of loose curls obscured one eye, and her smile needed one more tooth to complete the set.

"Hi, hon," she muttered.

"Hi, yourself. You Cindy?"

"Heck, no, hon. Gone for today." She turned to the pass-through behind her and grabbed two small salads. She balanced them on one arm, grabbed a bottle of A.1. with her other hand, and set off.

Through the opening, Alec could see the cook. He stood slope-shouldered, though he was tall and as wiry and thin as the waitress was not. His hair squirted out sideways from beneath his baseball cap. The cap, bill and all, looked as if food had been passed through rather than daubed on it over time. The red-and-purple pattern on his polyester vest warred with his yellow-and-blue Hawaiian shirt beneath it, top button open, blond tuft exposed.

The diner décor was early single-wide. A row of oakwood booths ran the length of the faux, one-time train car. Blue vinyl seats matched the counter stools where Alec sat. On a wall to his left, next to the "We reserve the right to refuse service to anyone" notice, hung a clock with numbers drunkenly scattered across its face above the inscription, "WHO CARES?" Scotch-taped prominently to the side of the cash register was a list of check kiters in twenty-four-point, bold. The suggestion box next to it had no slot. Across the way hung a photo of a blond model standing next to a '50s-something Ford station wagon captioned, "Get your woody serviced here."

Alec scanned the menu, not particularly hungry but needing to eat, then pivoted and assessed the clientele. Two good ol' boys wearing once-white T-shirts bent over their plates and fork-fisted chicken-fried steak, mashed potatoes, and gravy. They grunted as they ate, Alec couldn't tell whether in satisfaction or from the exertion.

At the next booth, a husband and wife sat motionless over cups of coffee and the remains of a meal. They looked out the window, engaged in the non-conversation of long-marrieds. Alec understood the silence, and, noting that both were going gray, understood how it had lasted.

In walked a geezer with a ZZ Top beard. He wore a Vietnam veteran's cap and leaned on a cane. His father, it had to be, shuffled along behind him, liver-spotted and wrinkled. They tottered past seated patrons, each feeble step possibly their last, until collective sighs rewarded their finally negotiating a booth.

Down the counter from Alec, a cowboy in worn overalls and a faded Pendleton shirt sat hunkered over his plate, talking on his cell phone. As the conversation went on, he'd shake his head and run a hand through wavy, black hair. Whatever the source of his consternation—it felt familiar, and Alec assumed it was female—he barked once more into the phone and jabbed it closed. He settled his Stetson back on his head.

A couple of youngsters at a corner table brightened the tableau. The boy, late teens, Alec guessed, had taken the trouble to wear a clean, short-sleeved, cotton shirt. His arms were tanned. His female companion had on a green tank top, white shorts, and tennis shoes—choices nicely complemented by her ponytail. Outside, the sky had begun to clear, and a glare of sunlight reflected off a parked car window and spotlit the youngsters like they were the focus of a movie shot.

Thinking he couldn't go wrong with a cheeseburger, Alec ordered one from "Not Cindy." While he waited, he assayed a collection of *objets d'art* hung on the walls, shellacked wood pictures for sale, each masterpiece a steal at $14.95. There were appliquéd photos of a bald eagle, an American flag, a pair of hands in prayer above a snippet from the Twenty-Third Psalm; also, a grizzly bear, a profile of JFK, and two shiny portraits of Elvis Presley (the young and the old). Oh, how his dad had loved The King. "You ain't nothin' but a hound dog" would come rolling down the hall from the shower before work in a clear baritone voice to his audience of shaking heads and grins at the breakfast table.

The burger turned out to be excellent. "California Dreamin'" drifted in from the kitchen, the cook's shoulders bopping in time. Alec's fingers tapped along. He looked up and in the reflection off the glass cabinet holding cream pies saw the teen couple's hands steal across and touch. Alec watched, absently rolling his wedding ring around on his finger. At the next table, the Old Marrieds smiled at each other and exchanged what seemed to be about three words, sufficient certainly after all the years of speaking paragraphs of unnecessary dialogue. "Roy and Earl" pushed back from their table, revealing satisfied abdomens that had taken years to perfect. They belched so simultaneously they had to be brothers and had the decency to grin. Down the way, Gramps and his son chuckled.

The lovelorn cowhand—a pretty safe bet—straightened his hat, tossed a bill on the counter, and left, punching in a number on his phone. The waitress watched him leave and shook her head. "He'll live," she opined. She turned to Alec. "Want dessert?"

"No thanks. Who did the artwork?" he asked.

"My daddy. Momma made him get a hobby. That or shoot him."

"I'll take one of the Elvises. The young one, with the guitar."

She made a show of wrapping the keepsake in butcher paper and securing it with twine.

Alec smiled and handed her a twenty. "Keep the change."

He paid for lunch, doubling the tip, and walked out into a perfect afternoon, artistic treasure cradled under his arm. Rain puddles reflected cirrus clouds and patches of blue. He fished out his keys, set Elvis across on the passenger seat, and climbed in.

His eyes caught the rearview mirror. "First, a shower," he said out loud.

The truck jumped to life.

Jubilate Canis
by Cynthia Tuell

(After Christopher Smart, "For His Cat, Jeoffry" from "Jubilate Agno.")

I will praise my dog Molly,
    for she is good!

Praise her in the morning and the evening;
Praise her in the 3:00 a.m. of my soul,
    for she curls her dogsbody asleep beside me;
    for her paws smell of the earth and her fur of the wilderness;
    for she counteracts the powers of darkness.

Praise her in her barking and in her restraint from barking;
Praise her in her sitting and in her lying down,
    for even as a pup—gamboling ball of electric fluff—she
        barked the stentorian bark of the righteous;
    yet she can practice discipline, quivering with urge but
        refraining;
    for she can constrain and swallow her yawps and chantingly
        sing like a sitar deep in her throat.

Praise her for her acuity,
    for she knows before the knock on the door, before the step
        on the porch, who is calling;
    for she keeps the Lord's watch against the adversary;
    for her ears arise, her nostrils twitch, she stands alertly still,
        every nerve alight;

for she breaks into dance to greet a friend on the threshold;
but when a stranger approaches she bristles and glares,
announcing, "Here is a dog! Beware!"

Praise her on fire roads and in canyons;
Praise her in the patches of snow,
for leashless she brisks about the Angeles;
for like her sister coyote she stalks the wild rodents and
bounds after the deer;
(for since she is well-fed, she will do no harm;)
for in springtime she saunters, curiously browsing the tall
grass, the lupine and paintbrush;
for she leaps, pirouetting midair above the buzz of the rattler,
while her prey, the squirrel, chatters high in the live oak
and over us all soars the hawk.

Praise her for her variety of acts,
for she shepherds the hiking children on the trail;
for she retrieves, points, races, hunts, determinedly digs,
harries the postman away with her bark and counteracts
the Devil, who is death;
for she is of the Tribe of Mutt, generations born of guileless
Nature's free selections and not by human will, for
human profit;
for she is a servant of the living God.

Praise Molly!
O praise her wholly ordinary name,
for she is of the Lord's poor and plentiful,
and every house is incomplete without her;
for she is of the common wealth—
doggy kisses and slaps of a jubilant tail;
a friend waggling with us down whatever road;
the sun prizing open the rim of the world at dawn,
faithfully filling Creation with light.

For Alexis
by Amanda Stubbert

That morning, our group of traveling writers had bounced our way out of Oaxaca proper in a white rental van to visit a local textile business still using traditional methods. As we pull off the dirt road (we'd left pavement fifteen minutes ago), a band of misfit authors follow Alberto, our Oaxacan guide in his signature crisp white shirt, like goslings into the courtyard brightly lit by the unimpeded sun. From the outside, this gated circle of three small buildings looks like an economical place you might go for a spare tire. Inside, however, we find every surface embedded with colorful, hand-painted tile. Doorways and window frames speak of folk tales I do not understand. Even the driveway is lined with colorful squares and shines up from our feet with moments of beauty.

This outing to the "textile place" as it was listed on our itinerary comes on day six of this trip curated for writers. Disruption is needed for truly new ideas and what better way to disrupt your thinking than travel? Shake off the ordinary and open your dulled senses? And yet, I almost skipped this particular chance at adventure. Yesterday was a lot. We trooped around the painstakingly restored, pre-Columbian city square, Monte Albán, in the blaring sun. Our German tour guide chastised anyone who dared step away for a photo or a bit of shade. Though we jumped at her spicy commands, treating us as wayward children versus paying customers, Brunhilda did relay some interesting facts. The tidbit I continue to chew on relates to how the city's inhabitants housed their dead. Though priests and royalty were buried in the temple, the bones of everyday folks rested in a crypt built into the corner of each family home. Presumably serving as a daily reminder of who came before you and upon whose shoulders you stood.

But this morning, our leader who has experienced a textile tour before, promised us "magic," and, cynical or not, we want to see.

Alberto, whose small stature matches my own, ushers us toward an alcove, a frontage of the building to our left. He flashes his radiant smile I wish I could match with my own, and explains our time here will begin with a demonstration. As we choose from an eclectic set of chairs, my eye travels to the corner of the stone-and-brick structure of this rug business, guessing at whether or not bones lay within. At our feet lies a color wheel of woolen yarn. Behind each bundle of thread sits a traditional bowl holding the key ingredient for producing each hue. Daniel, the stately leader of his family business at a mere thirty-nine, takes his seat at the center of this educational semicircle. We can hear the sound of others working within the structures edging the courtyard, but, as if to force our focus now on Daniel in his dusty jeans and gray sweatshirt, no one else appears. Our class takes place with Daniel's practiced speech in Spanish pausing at regular intervals for Alberto to catch us up in English.

Daniel explains how his family, thirty-eight members in all, are involved in the business somewhere between shearing the sheep and selling the finished product. I begin to ask if all thirty-eight live on this land, but don't want to interrupt, so I stay silent.

Daniel shows us how to card the wool with the same needled paddles used for centuries, and allows the novel-writing philosophy professor to have a go, demonstrating the difficulty of the task he made look so easy. Next, our teacher steps up to the spinning wheel, turning the carded fluff into yarn as if returning the material to its original form. He does not ask for volunteers this time, because we see the technique requires extreme precision and have no need for further proof of this.

We move on to the colors. Green is created from various kinds of moss and limestone paste. The paste Daniel holds appears stark white, yet turns the yarn a vibrant green. Yellows come by soaking the yarn with chamomile twigs. Orange from pomegranate skins and marigold petals. Shades of brown are accomplished by using both brown sheep's wool and walnut shells. All interesting, but not yet magic. I check the wall once more for any signs of ancestors.

As our host takes questions about the dyeing process, a little boy in a brown hoodie, skinny jeans, and Vans appears with a tray holding shot glass mugs of hot chocolate. Alberto explains that this is Daniel's son, Alexis, and that the chocolate is handmade by the matriarch of the family. The medical doctor writing about climate change attempts to engage our tiny waiter in conversation about the proffered beverage.

"*¿Tu abuela hizo esto?*"

"Oh," Alberto shakes his head, "he does not speak Spanish. He speaks Zapotec, the local, pre-Hispanic language."

I don't want hot chocolate, I'm lactose intolerant. But when Alexis's round face, using all his concentration to not slosh our beverages, turns up to mine and his veil of thick eyelashes women would pay money for lifts to reveal his shining eyes filled with joy, innocence, and hope, I can't say no. I smile and nod a *gracias*. My one sip brings a grainy texture I was not expecting, and, as Alexis disappears back inside, I set the mug gently at my feet.

Then Daniel gets to the color red. He pulls out a ping-pong paddle cactus leaf covered in white specks. He explains that each dot is a bug, a parasite. Specific cacti are used for farming the insect, left to feed and grow exactly ninety days. If harvested too early, the bugs won't be large enough and if left a moment longer, will kill their gracious host. Daniel plucks one mite from the green pad. Then, with the flourish of a Vegas illusionist, he brushes his left thumb across his right palm and the white speck becomes a handful of brilliant red.

We tourists ooh and ahh. We are converts. We say, "We now see the magic."

Daniel smiles, no need for translation. He has performed this act before. And he is not finished. Squeezing a wedge of fresh lime above his hand like a celebrity chef above a sauté pan, the drops of juice turn his red palm bright orange.

We clap. Is there more?

Daniel dips the tip of his finger into the dish of stark white limestone paste.

"What will this create?" Daniel asks us with his eyebrows.

We call out guesses. No one is correct. Swallowing our choices, we watch his palm become a rich, plum purple.

"Blue," Daniel explains through Alberto, "is the most difficult color to achieve." Each of us holds out our hands to receive what appear to be lightweight lumps of coal. This is indigo. A special tree found only in a specific coastal region of Mexico contains a sap which, if boiled out of the branches, mixed with ash, and allowed to dry in the sun produces these precious nuggets we now hold.

"Do the rugs with lots of blue cost more?" asks the army vet.

Daniel replies, wobbling his hand back and forth as if to say *a bit*.

Alberto jumps in with: "The price is mostly determined by the hours taken for weaving."

With that, our troop crosses the courtyard to a curtained-off, three-sided carport-sized housing four looms, each the size of an elevator car.

Daniel steps up to the pipe organ pedals and demonstrates how to operate the machine, and through translation, we learn that each rug or cloth must be completed by the same artisan who began. The strength of each lever pull is unique to the individual, and any change will be detectable in the finished product.

Our American sensibilities jump to timeframes.

"How long does a four-by-six-foot rug take to weave?"

"About sixty days of eight-hour labor."

"How long to set up the loom for a new project?"

"About two weeks."

We do the math and shake our heads. We've been softened by a life of instant gratification and reel at the thought of such a labor-intensive process.

The millennial, a visual artist, speaks up, inquiring about the patterns.

"If the rug is an art piece," Alberto translates, "they draw the pattern on the base strings. But for traditional patterns, they just execute, follow their hands."

The Westerners exchange more astonished glances, unable to fathom how one could create such intricate and symmetrical designs without a blueprint.

As we head back across the open courtyard once more, we make a quick detour to see the kiddie-pool-sized vat for boiling and dyeing the yarn. Our host points out an iron hook-and-pulley system used to extract the heavy, water-logged material. Even the water must be purchased or collected or gathered. Nothing comes easily here, nothing quickly.

The contents of the store/gallery hold a new weight now that we have knowledge of their origins, the exertion and industry baked within each piece. Rugs of all sizes hang on the walls and lay in stacks around the room. Another semicircle of chairs awaits our arrival, and as we sit, hand-painted gourd-halves are placed in our hands. Alberto pours a tablespoon of golden alcohol into each cup, the aroma of this bright mezcal the latest magic trick.

"What is this?" I call to Alberto as he continues to fill cups.

Daniel laughs. Apparently, I am not the first to be struck by this libation.

Alberto laughs too. "Do you like it?"

"I think the smell alone could heal the sick!"

"Their family mezcal. They make it here. With several flavors."

But I don't care about the other flavors. This bottled sunshine may be the best liquor I've ever tasted. Perhaps the best *liquid* I've ever tasted. I have discovered joy in a glass.

When Alberto has filled all of the glasses, mine is empty and I ask if I am allowed more. His twinkling eyes say yes, and my glass is full once more.

Plucking one rug after another from various piles, Daniel shows us traditional patterns, modern patterns, and art pieces, while describing how to care for the rugs that should last for a lifetime. Our heads bobble back and forth, wishing to appear attentive to our host and hear Alberto's translations at the same time. Daniel points out motifs in the traditional designs, explaining how they represent mountains, trees, familial generations.

When we are released to explore on our own, we make one discovery after another. Coasters made by children learning the trade, basically three-by-four-inch rugs, selling for twenty dollars apiece. I consider purchasing two, one for each of my children, but . . . would they appreciate the souvenirs' significance? Probably not. Next, I come across clutches, coin purses and tote bags. These would certainly get more day-to-day use, but I have a hard time paying the price. I know the items are *worth* much more than the tags ask for, and yet my thrift wins out and I move on.

Eventually, I begin to dread leaving as a group without purchasing our fair share, without serving as patrons to these lovely craftspeople keeping the ancient alive. But soon I notice shopping bags appearing in the hands of one group member after another. Inside are rugs, runners, and scarves. Once, I turn to see the millennial wearing a rust-colored cape reminiscent of *The Little Match Girl* and go in search of a similar garment in another pattern. I lay my hands on a gloriously soft, gray-and-white patterned poncho with a rolled collar and hand-hewn wooden buttons. I'm in love. One by one we all find a new *amor* in this speed-dating event. There is, indeed, something for everyone.

With the monetary ice thus broken, I ask Alberto if the sunshine in a glass that has liberated my peace and my credit card is for sale. He says yes, of course. But when he translates my wishes to Daniel's pint-sized wife, the cashier, she does not look as happy about the idea. After a back and forth between spouses, they ask Alberto to explain that they have only one remaining, unopened bottle.

The next exchange in Zapotec I can translate myself. If she is to relinquish her last full bottle, I will have to pay a higher price. But what will that price be? Suddenly, I feel less like a good customer and more like a dinner guest asking to buy the placemats. Should I relent? Let the family keep the mezcal purchased from the neighboring farm and steeped in pomegranate rinds which they use to loosen every tourist's inhibition and purse strings? No,

I will wait for the price and pay it, if I can. This juice of the gods must be shared back home where earth-tethered delight is all too rare.

They agree to take two thousand pesos, about one hundred dollars, and I happily hand over my plastic currency. My husband will forgive me this excess when the cure-all elixir meets his tongue.

Alexis appears again holding a cordless phone. His mother takes the handset and converses, while Alexis whispers something to his dad. Daniel smiles and brings out a two-by-three-foot rug filled with blocks of vivid colors. Alexis has made this rug and wants us to see it. We all convey our pleasure, our awe at his mature technique, yet no one steps up to add his creation to their bulging bags. Where in my small, highly curated apartment would I house such an item? One by one, we apologize for leaving Alexis's rug behind. His brave and gracious acceptance leaves a tiny chink in my armor of happiness.

Lunch is the final item on our agenda. This family business does not generally feed tourists or local customers, Alberto explains, but they are friends of his and will allow us to share the family's lunch. We literally pull back the curtain to the private family space, the carport area housing the communal dining room/kitchen. Our small traveling band takes up every white plastic stacking chair around the two folding tables covered with a cotton cloth as remarkable as the wool folded into our carryalls. The *abuela* offers what appears to be her stool used for cooking over the charcoal hibachi to Alberto who then sits next to me, the table hitting him just below the shoulders.

The feast before us fits on a bread plate: Half of a corn tortilla made moments ago on the *chimeneas*, a flat square of beef about the size of an index card and a fried slice of cactus to match, one hunk of cauliflower, one of broccoli, and two wedges of zucchini. On the table is a cereal bowl of fresh lettuce and tomatoes, the richest red I have ever seen, to pass, family-style. I'm used to American portions and assume this bounty is merely the first course, but the whole food magically fills our stomachs. We are thoroughly satisfied.

Each of us sighs with contentment, assuming we have savored every bite of this experience, when the *abuela* whips a piece of cloth off a ski jump-shaped mortar and pestle. She slides a flat candle underneath as heating the stone makes the surface smooth for grinding. Then, as if our travel diaries are not already over-flowing, she proceeds to create chocolate for our dessert. Scraped fresh from the stone, our digestif made of fresh cacao and cinna-mon, tastes grainy, earthy, and somehow wholesome. Abuela performs the final illusion, producing a bowl with hunks of her finished product and wallets appear once more; our bulging satch-els find room for one bit more.

Something has shifted. Our group smiles to each other, won-dering if our fellow travelers are feeling the same change in the air. We beam to our hosts, hoping to convey our gratitude beyond the word *gracias*. This family has not simply demonstrated their work for us, not simply produced goods we will use as dinner party conversation back home. This family has opened their arms and let us in, shared a perspective of connection with history and land we Westerners only read about. We've seen through new eyes and will never be the same. Disruption has occurred and I know, somehow, I will bring a piece of Oaxaca with me wherever I go.

We shuffle toward our van, full in mind, body, and spirit, not quite ready to leave, each asking permission to return on our own someday. Daniel and Abuela, through Alberto, say we are welcome anytime. Alexis tugs on his father's hand and asks a question which is related to Alberto and back. A three-way game of catch with a language ball.

Alberto's always genuine smile grows an extra glint. "I explained to him that you are all writers. He wants to know if one of you will write about him and his family so they might become famous."

As tears wet my eyes, I turn to my fellow authors and relay the child's request.

"Yes," I say, bending to meet Alexis face-to-face. "Yes, I promise I will write about you and about our day with your family."

As I climb into the van, I continue to mentally answer his question . . .

Will I write about you, Alexis? How could I keep from retelling our meeting to others? The picture of your family's deep roots in this land and each other burns within me like the embers of your clay oven. You have put the very earth beneath my feet and sunshine in my hands. Will I write about you? Not only that. I will keep the bones of your memory in the corner of my mind always remembering your contribution to your culture and to my journey.

Will I write about you, Alexis? Sí. In these pages and within the walls of my heart.

Psalm 100 Illuminated for People Living Near the Salish Sea by Carla Shafer

Make the bark of the seal
deep from your abdomen
and feel vibrations of joy—

Serve creation as if you are sunlight
radiating from the wingtip
of a soaring, glaucous gull—

Know your breath from its first
intake and release and
remember all the ones ignored

Know each fiber of your body
and the rhythm of your thoughts given only to you
freely, unconditionally—

Enter into waters where salmon swim
in conversation with the Spirit, from which all is
made possible, with praise and song—

For you are blessed and this bounteous life you receive
unfolds renewable as the seasons in every seed and fruit,
and in every drop of rain touching your skin.

Lila
by Susan Chase-Foster

By the third May of the pandemic, our garden looked impossibly green, as if it had been photoshopped. Out in the backyard, weeding our longest raised bed under charcoal skies and intermittent drizzles, I worked my *hori hori* knife through dirt dappled with a universe of unwanted mountain ash seedlings.

At the far end of the bed, in a corner formed by a cedar fence and *torii* gate, a massive twin-trunked lilac grew. Old enough to bear shaggy bark and white lichen beards on contorted, moss-cloaked branches, the lilac resembled a woodblock print of an ancient, gnarled tree one might find in a book of Japanese art or folktales. During full moons, the lilac looked more like two bent old women in tattered sweaters leaning on walking sticks than it did a tree.

We guessed the lilac was at least a hundred years old, planted in 1922 the year our Craftsman home was built. Another possibility was that the tree was much older, blown in as a seed from a mother lilac on the grounds of the Roeder Home, a Gothic-American mansion in whose shadow our back garden lies.

Because I too am old, after an hour my back ached from bending over. I set my knife and self on the wooden rim of the bed and gazed up. On recent walks in our neighborhood, I'd observed an abundance of lilac blossoms. I'd inhaled their intoxicating, almost overwhelmingly sweet scent. But our lilac, though crowned with vibrant green, heart-shaped leaves, did not appear to have a speck of purple or pink or white anywhere, or even a hint of perfume. I was stunned. Was the lilac a late bloomer? Diseased? Infected by coronavirus? Or was this just the beginning of the end?

I plodded to the front yard where my husband busied himself nail-gunning recycled wood onto the remodel of our porch. He turned off the air compressor's rhythmic gasps when he saw me, smiled, waited for me to say something.

"You know the lilac in the back near the *torii* gate?"

"Yep."

"I think it's dying. We might need to, you know, take it out."

He frowned, looked at me as if, at seventy-five, I'd just announced, "Guess what? I'm pregnant."

"It's not blooming like all the other lilacs around here. *Nada.* I think it might be too old. Maybe we should replace it with a new one."

He stared at me.

My words echoed through the Elder Lives Matter lobes of my brain: *Not blooming. Too old. Take it out. Replace it with a new one.* Holy shit, what if someone said that about me? I would be outraged. Wounded.

My husband tightened his lips, raised his eyebrows, and gave me enough time to birth an epiphany.

"I'm going to take another look," I told him. "Maybe my death sentence is premature."

"Good plan, Stan." He fired up his air compressor, shot a few nails from his gun.

I walked to the far back of the garden, grabbed a plastic lawn chair along the way, positioned it under the lilac and plunked myself down. I gazed up through the lilac into the distant sky. My mind was blank, empty, perhaps in a state of *boketto*, a Japanese word I'd discovered for staring vacantly into space without thinking. Something I practiced frequently, when I should have been writing.

After a while, I noticed that the garden seemed unusually still. Silence replaced the chatter of resident crows, gulls, and black-capped chickadees. The air felt calm, neither cold nor warm. The sky glowed with splotches of baby blue. I looked deep into the lilac. My eyes roamed like a drone inspecting every branch, each leaf. I gasped. Above me, a thousand backlit hearts in shades of emerald, lime, kiwi, and jade shimmered. Everywhere, clusters of pale lavender blossoms trembled and waved like prayer flags. I inhaled the scent of lilac and giggled like a child.

This has to be legerdemain, but by whose hand? With the next beat of my heart, I heard a whispered, *"Lila,"* the Spanish word for lilac. I stood up, placed my hands on one of the lilac's bent lower limbs. She—for her name implied femininity—felt rough, a bit tousled, but warm, and welcoming, and beautiful.

"Tree, did you just tell me your name is Lila?"

A sudden breeze flurried purple blossoms into my lap. This is how I came to realize our lilac's name, and that she was a sentient being who, though old, was very much alive.

From then on, I began to hang out with Lila most days. I moved a small stone statue of Guan Yin, Bodhisattva of Compassion and Kindness, next to my new friend to keep her company when I was away, and set a candle at her base to light during each visit.

In the beginning, I simply sat under Lila's canopy, studied her branches and twigs, leaves and blossoms dancing with the wind. I wrote notes in my journal.

Quite a show-off, Lila shimmies and shudders or whips wildly until her blossoms fall on me. She is rarely still.

Today, Lila executes a spectacular pas de trois with both the kiwi (through whose trellis she pokes), and downbed, the mountain ash. A few times, I join them when I think no one is looking.

On a windless day, I began to read to Lila. Whitman's pastoral elegy, "When Lilacs Last in the Dooryard Bloom'd" made both of us sad. I lowered my head. Lila drooped a few lower branches until one rested on my shoulder. Another day, as I read the words "You are everywhere," from Amy Lowell's poem "Lilacs," Lila reached up toward the powerlines in an arboreal gesture of elation. I copied her by stretching my arms up and up until I feared I might fall backwards. Being old, my balance had waned a bit, and so had Lila's; her large limbs seemed to have leaned lower over time.

When the weather warmed, we moved on to Kate Chopin's *Lilacs and Other Stories*. Lila's favorite was the title tale, if spontaneous, euphonic creaks were a measure. I agreed.

About then, I realized how a lilac, perhaps any tree, could be the bearer of messages. Upon reading, "What are you writing now?" in the preface from *The Lilac Fairy Book*, I moaned. That very second, Lila hurled a small branch festooned with blossoms at my feet. Was this a gift of compassion? A not-so-gentle poke at a writer on unreasonably long respite? I think perhaps both. Which is why from then on, during each visit, I made a point of writing something in my journal and reading it aloud while Lila watched and listened over me. If she was pleased, which was almost always the case, she'd swish her branches and fill the air with sweet perfume.

At the peak of summer, Lila began speaking to me in light.

Today is the warmest day of the year. Heat and humidity are having a soporific effect on me. Though, as I read from Richard Powers' delightful The Overstory, a constant drone of bees buzzing around the dregs of Lila's blossoms keeps me awake. "There are trees that spark like fireworks and trees that rise like . . ."

At that moment, in what appeared to be sun bursting through gaps in Lila's canopy, a frenetic, chiaroscuro spectacle of light orbs and shadow fluttered across the page.

But how can there be fluttering? There is absolutely no wind!

Using the language of light, Lila seemed to be saying, "I am one of those who sparks like fireworks."

All I could do was hug my lilac and tell her, "I know you are."

As the weather turned blustery, Lila's leaves began to brown and drop. I bundled up and we continued to work our way through Andrew Lang's *The Lilac Fairy Book.* Of course, none of the stories had anything to do with lilacs, but I believed Lila adored the deep purple cover of a knight slaying a dragon, and, not to brag, the irresistibly engaging sound of my voice as I took on the various good or evil characters.

Lila rustles, a sound reminiscent of paper pompoms we used to shake at high school football games. I kneel down, hug her two trunks, warm and comforting in this cold place, though scratchy against my hands. A moldy mixture of damp leaves and wet dirt has replaced her dulcet scent.

I am so in love with this tree!

By late fall, in her shaggy gray bark and fresh tufts of moss, leafless Lila looked ancient. More than ever, she resembled two old women bent with arthritis, shivering in the rain. But I wasn't sad. After all, she'd survived at least one hundred Pacific Northwest winters. Even with the meteorological uncertainty of global warming, I felt certain she'd survive this one too, and be back in full bloom come spring. Maybe not as early as some lilacs, being an elder tree, but soon after.

The first snow of winter dumped two feet of snow on our garden and knocked off a couple of succulents and a yearling wisteria. Everyone else, plant-wise, seemed fine. Lila looked gorgeous in her fluffy white shawl.

But the night before Christmas Eve, a downpour of freezing rain covered our world in thick glass. The following morning, we were to drive up to the Sunshine Coast of British Columbia to be with our children for the holiday. At dawn, in his hiking boots, wool cap, and heaviest parka, my husband tromped out back to warm our Subaru, which was parked under Lila.

What he found was shocking. One of Lila's thickest limbs, weighted down with snow and ice had twisted, fractured, broken away from the trunk, and landed on the back of the car. In order to drive out, he had to saw the massive limb into smaller chunks and drag them out into the alley behind the *torii* gate.

Before we headed north, we walked out back together to take a look at the damage to our dear tree. Lila stood in the cold, with what remained of her broken limb protruding like an amputation without its prosthesis. We felt numb, and then we cried.

"Merry Christmas," we wished Lila as we tied a sheaf of holly and ivy to a branch close to her wound with a red ribbon.

In the weeks post-Christmas, I made short visits to Lila daily, although it was too cold to read to her. Instead, I burned incense and covered her open wound with an old beret. I sniffed her bark, fondled her lichen, and brushed my hand along her moss. My husband cut two twigs bearing buds from her downed limb and placed each in a glass of water on our kitchen windowsill.

"Just in case," he said.

She may die, he's thinking. I am too. What should we do? Should we prune Lila back to a wisp of herself? Should we call an arborist to remove her entirely? Is it time to say goodbye?

In the middle of the night on New Year's Day, the answer came to me in a dream that included a theater marquee flashing "The Agony in the Garden" in brilliant green-and-purple lights:

Do not terminate your tree's life.
That's not your job.
Trim her severed limb close to the trunk.
Level the surface to make a little table for burning incense.
On her branches, hang a high-pitched wind chime and other wind toys.
When spring arrives, plant her babies under her.
And by all means, continue reading to Lila. She's a literary lilac!

It is now mid-January. Lila is decked out in a new purple wind chime, very high-pitched, as directed in the dream. A lavender wind carp sways in the winter wind. Lilac incense wafts from a wooden burner set on the tiny table my husband made from what remained of her lost limb. Still too cold to read to Lila, I bundled up and told her the story of how Pan, the Greek god of forests and fields, chased the wood nymph, Syringa, until out of fear she turned herself into a lilac. When Pan discovered Syringa in her new form, he used one of her branches to create the first panpipe, an instrument with a very high pitch.

"Like your wind chime, Lila," I said, pinging the purple tubes with my hand.

When the weather warms up, possibly around May in the fourth year of the pandemic, we'll take Lila's seedlings, now nicely bursting with buds in their glass jars on the kitchen windowsill, and plant them under their mom. In that way, Lila may continue to live for another hundred years, or maybe more.

A Seasonal Prayer
by Sky Hedman

Paint me a forest path, level and worn.
Put it on the far side over
A sturdy wooden bridge.
Safe passage across the noisy creek.
Make the path wide enough for each of us.
I can pass you with a word.
You return to me a nod.
Make the people friendly.
Those with their dogs
Or their familiars
Or alone.

Fill in the border on either side
With brushy vegetation.
Pervasive yellow flowers on top of long stems.
Oval leaves amid tassels of tall grass.
Layer it with resurgent blackberry stalks.

Let the thick grove of trees throw patches of shade.
Have them absorb the sounds of distant traffic.
Show the dappled alder trunks, the cedar boughs
The furrowed trunks of Douglas firs.
Let them grow this forest.

Make it June.
Listen to songbirds.
The upward cascade of Swainson's thrush.
The insistent drilling of woodpeckers.
Or young ravens
Squawking raucously,
Unseen in the high canopy.

After months of subdued gray,
Make the sun shine.
Yet keep the air cool
To my flannelled arms.
Let my dog trot before me,
Ears flapping, eyes alert,
Pausing to sniff undetectable delights.

I cannot paint peace,
But what I feel
I'll sketch for you with words.
Let me feel all this love.
Let me share it with you.

Finding a Way Home
by Sheila Dearden

Imagine this. Salmon carry a map of home wrapped within the double helix of their DNA, their body the compass. In the fall they gather at the mouths of summer-parched rivers and creeks, waiting for the first flush of cooling rain so they can continue upstream to spawn and die. Over winter, the pink, pea-sized eggs are nested in the river-washed gravel and come spring, salmon fry, no bigger than a child's pinkie, drift with the current, imprinting the rocks, soils, and plants of home, mapping the signature scent of their natal stream. They grow from fry to smolt and follow the current downstream to the estuary where they adapt to brackish water before riding out on saltwater tides as sleek, young adults. Magnetite crystals within the tissues of their quicksilver bodies attune to the earth's magnetic field, lock the coordinates of this transition point. The salmon version of pinning location. Swimming the Pacific Ocean for three, four, or five years, eventually, they are drawn homeward, to their natal stream where they will spawn and die. The cycle continues as it has for thousands of years. Commitment to place shapes salmon lives from the moment of their hatching to their dying. Their bodies are uniquely sized and muscled for their particular spawning journey, whether it be upstream in coastal rivers, creeks, or to headwaters of major rivers a thousand miles inland from the Pacific Ocean.

And yet, salmon remain open to possibility. A biological impulse that drove them to explore freshwater ice-melt in the wake of retreating glaciers thousands of years ago remains encoded in their genes. Six years ago, two outdated dams were dismantled on the Elwha River. Within two years of the river waters flowing freely from snowfields in the Olympic Mountains to the Strait of Juan de Fuca, salmon returned to spawn in habitat that dams had prevented them from reaching for almost one hundred years. With singularity of purpose, they found a way home.

Home. I say the word out loud, feel it start as a sigh in the lungs, end as a hum on the lips. I could be chanting a series of "oms" for the weight of belonging it engenders.

Home for me was England where I was born and spent my childhood in one place, one house, where, according to my mother, getting insufficient fresh air or being underfoot when she was doing the housework were cardinal sins. I was banished outdoors to play, the only requirements being to stay out of trouble and be home for meals. I was a free-range child imprinting hills, woods and wildflower meadows. Bluebells, cowslips, cuckoos, hedgehogs, skylarks, song thrushes were my magnetite crystals pinning me home.

I met my husband in college. Steve had just returned from a summer on the west coast of America and had fallen in love with a landscape that still held traces of the wild west in his imagination. A handful of years after we graduated, a job opportunity in the Pacific Northwest presented itself, a temporary adventure, I thought, no more than two years. We arrived in Washington State on a rainy July day. I was no stranger to rain, but in this drearily gray place surrounded by dark, densely packed evergreen trees with broomstick tops tangled in clouds I felt no connection to landscape or place.

We had been living in Washington State for a little over a year and I was eight months pregnant with my son when I first saw salmon. My parents were visiting from England to welcome their first grandchild. On a periwinkle-blue October day, the three of us decided lunch outdoors would be perfect. We found a restaurant with tables outside, placed our order, and were enjoying a cup of coffee when we heard splashing from behind the thicket of vegetation concealing a creek. "Ducks," my mother declared, while my father walked along the boardwalk to investigate. Within moments he was back, urging us to take a look. We followed, a little reluctantly. Me, because of my belly, my mother, for having to leave her coffee and chair in the sunshine. We reached the viewing platform in time to see three large, bronzed fish splashing over the shallow gravel bar and sliding into shadows beneath the overhanging bank. "I think they're salmon," my father announced. When the waitress delivered our food, she confirmed his guess. "There's a fish hatchery upstream," she explained. "They're chinook salmon returning to spawn. Not unlike yourself," her eyes implied as she glanced at my very pregnant belly.

A year later, just before my son's first birthday, I would discover chinook salmon in our local stream. By the time my son was four, my daughter, two, it would have become a tradition to celebrate the return of salmon each fall. Over time, I would uncover the ecology of this place. I would read about old growth forests with evergreen trees so vast it took twelve sets of outstretched arms to encircle their trunks. I'd go hiking and find trees old enough to have been seedlings when the Magna Carta was signed and just reaching maturity when the Mayflower nosed into Plymouth Bay. I would learn that salmon were threads that wove together ocean, rivers, and forest.

Thirty-five salmon seasons have passed since that first encounter. Salmon have stitched me in place. To bluebells, cowslips, cuckoos, hedgehogs, skylarks, song thrushes that pinned me to my childhood home, I now include salmon, orca, gray whales, black bears, Swainson's thrushes, hummingbirds as the magnetite crystals orienting me home in the Pacific Northwest.

On a beautiful June day, I take my cup of tea outside and savor the warmth of a morning sun drawing lacy tree-shadows over the field in front of my house. A Swainson's thrush calls from the maples. An ascending, fluting melody that winds like a prayer flag through the trees and sings of the returning salmon and Southern Resident orca to the Salish Sea.

Just about every year since our children were babies, we have travelled to the San Juan Islands in May or June to welcome whales. At Lime Kiln Point State Park, we would stand on barnacle-encrusted rocks at the water's edge, clutching the children's hands as we watched orca entwined in kelp breathing on the surface. When they were ten and twelve, we acquired two double kayaks and would paddle along the rocky tideline finding sea stars, crabs, anemone, and most years, glimpses of whales, way out on the water.

Our son and daughter are adults now with busy lives and are not so available. This year, only Steve and I respond to the Swainson's song and the promise of whales. We load the car, catch the ferry to a launch site on San Juan Island where we slither over seaweed-slickened rocks with the two-person kayak slung between us to reach the water's edge. Gasping at the cold ache of water on our feet, we clamber into the boat, cinch spray skirts, and push away from the shore. We know with a deep animal sense of knowing that we do not choose encounters, the whales do. Out on the water, I carry with me a quiet yearning to be chosen.

The day starts like so many others, cool morning air and a sun gleaming like a pearl in the mist. My senses are scrambled in this mercurial world where sea and sky are indiscernible. Needing an anchor point, I stir ripples on the surface to restore water and sky to their rightful place. A warming sun slowly tears the mist to shreds, tints the sea blue-green. The shadowy outline of a harbor seal weaves through the eel grass beneath our kayaks, then disappears as we head toward deep water and a steeply pitched shoreline fringed with swirling blades of kelp. We round a rocky point just as a curtain of whale breath is drawn across the sea, black blade dorsal fins of orcas cutting toward us some distance ahead. They disappear in unison. We head toward shore to avoid being an unnecessary obstacle, hearts thrumming with excitement, apprehension. Reaching the relative safety of the kelp bed, my husband unhooks his spray skirt and reaches into the cockpit to retrieve his camera from its storage case. I peer over the edge of the kayak only to see my reflected face distorted into a rippling, ghoulish mask. The sea remains a quiet expanse interrupted only by the fluting of a distant thrush.

Suddenly, the surface explodes and a whale slides so close to our kayak we can see the flare of her nostril bellowing breath from cavernous lungs. Her dorsal fin cuts the water, spindrift streaming over gray saddle patch and raven-black back. The kayak sways precariously as much from our startlement as from the wash of the orca's body. Instinctively, I flex my hand flat-palmed toward the water as if I can conjure a firm surface against which to steady myself. Everywhere is noise and streaming water as the sea bursts to five more blowholes, explosive orca exhalations, and the sound of wild clicking. I glance over my shoulder to see my husband has managed to extricate his camera and is now fumbling to focus as the tip of an adult male's dorsal fin grows out of the water to tower six feet above us. Three, four, five more breaths, the whales disappear below the surface. We rock over their whirlpool footprints as Steve juggles his camera and the neoprene bag containing the hydrophones. We scramble to insert earbuds and lower the hydrophones into the water so we can eavesdrop on the chorus of whistles, clicks, and sighs as they speak of their underwater world. Their conversation fades and we watch them surface in the distance, disappear beyond the point.

Slowly, the world around us slips back into focus. Steve and I look at each other and laugh in delight, in disbelief. I'm struck by a memory. "Do you remember that day at Lime Kiln Point years ago when Megan was three years old?" I ask, "When a male orca surfaced right next to a raft of kayakers just beyond the kelp bed and we heard one of them yell, 'holy shit,' across the water? And after that, every time Megan saw a whale that day she pointed and said, 'holy shit.' So proud of her new words!" We both laugh as Steve adds, "Yes! And I think we've just had our own 'holy shit' moment."

As Steve is stowing his camera in its case and the hydrophones back in the cockpit, I listen to gulls braying close by, watch a bald eagle sailing on broad wings high overhead. I think of the salmon hiding in the dark waters below us. Every part of their life journey from egg to spawning adult is fraught with danger. Orcas and bald eagles are just two of the more than one hundred and thirty-five species that depend on salmon as part of their diet.

My gaze drifts back to the bald eagle and I try to picture the view from a bird's eye perspective. The Salish Sea spread out in the shape of a lung whose bronchi, bronchioles, alveoli are the freshwater rivers, creeks, lakes. Freshwater out-breath from rivers delivers oxygen, minerals, and organic forest matter that mixes into a nutrient-dense stew. With every tidal saltwater in-breath microscopic diatoms and plankton feed the wriggling, reaching, gulping tentacles, claws, mouths of countless barnacles, anemone, tube worms, crustaceans, shellfish, sea stars; fish who in turn are scooped, plucked, crunched by otters, seals, porpoises, salmon, birds, dolphins, whales.

One hundred and fifty years ago, a bird would have looked down on old growth forests, vast wetlands, and wild rivers running free. Today, the bald eagle soars over a densely populated area with more than eight million people living on islands and the surrounding mainland. Many of the rivers have been dammed for hydropower or irrigation. Much of the land paved, logged, drained, resulting in the depletion of once abundant animal and plant communities. Even in the brief time I have lived here I have witnessed a decline in the Southern Resident orca population, the loss of local salmon runs.

Just beyond the kelp, a sleek seal head slides out of the water, pewter-gray dog nose angled toward us, nostrils flared, he inhales our presence. Onyx eyes fix our gaze as if to say, pay attention. We are still here. Salmon, orca, seals, bald eagles. He sinks into the depths, leaving a slice of hope that life has the regenerative capacity to flourish. It remains up to us to summon the will to live more lightly on the Earth. To find the courage to cherish and protect this wondrous world. And, to let home make salmon of us all.

The Devotion of Apple Blossoms
by Victoria Doerper

Infinite faith is required
To sense green in the world
When all is bare sticks and brown
And a cold wind wreaking havoc with
Boughs and branches.
But that's the job of buds
Meditating in their little cells,
Solemn for a season or two,
Until sun and warmth
Loosen chaste sepals,
Ignite a holy passion
Of color and fragrance,
A tender fluttering
As they give themselves away
To bees and hummingbirds,
Wild spring breezes,
Butterflies,
The eyes of passersby,
And in final perfect offering,
Abandoning all else,
A gentle swelling into fruit.

Snakeskin
by Victoria Doerper

I see the signs of scales
On the sand. A snake
Has been here, sliding
And slithering, and not
Comfortable, old skin
Not conforming to the new
Being. Stuck in a skin
That does not fit.
But snakes can wriggle
Out of the old covering,
Leaving behind parasites
And the skin of yesterdays.
And I imagine I can too,
The letting go, the patience,
The moving forward
And leaving the past behind,
Light as dust,
For the wind to carry away.

Orchid
by Victoria Doerper

I admire her
My kitchen orchid.
I don't actually know
If she's a she
Though I've always
Thought of her that way.
Not because of her beauty
But rather her toleration
For neglect,
Her toughness that fights
Against constraint
Causes her to upend things
Push her roots out into the air
When the tiny pot
Stifles growth below.
I am no fit gardener
But she carries on
Despite the lack
Of proper care
And while I ignore her
She creates a long stalk
Swelling with buds.
I admire her
Determination
To flower.

Driveway Day
by Katie Fleischmann

I have metastatic breast cancer. I am living with incurable cancer that is currently managed with medication. I'm still not sure how to say this out loud to fully portray the hugeness of it without sounding grim. Treatment has taken a toll on me, but I still have this life to live. I still have a daughter to raise and to show how to do this awful, hopeful, scary, beautiful thing we call life.

When my daughter was small, I made a pact that we would get outside every day. Some days it's the short walk to the mailbox, others it's a long hike in the woods or a bike ride by the marina. Today is a perfect driveway day. Early spring, and the sun is out but it isn't quite warm yet. I pull out a lawn chair, the old-school kind with plastic, woven webbing that gets looser and looser with each use and I question whether today's the day I'm going to fall through. But it's bright pink and orange: happy colors.

"Can I do chalk?" my daughter calls from somewhere in the garage.

"Sure," I yell back as I push myself out of my happy chair for the third time since I got it out ten minutes ago. I grab the half-empty tub of broken sidewalk chalk from the shelf and take it out to the driveway, then head back to my chair. My daughter is four.

I should know by now that I can't just sit and enjoy a sunny afternoon and get lost in my thoughts, but I sit down again as she starts to doodle.

"Mom, do you want to draw with me?"

No. My forty-year-old, cancer-wrecked body doesn't want to crawl around on the concrete and draw a kitty or a bunny or a dog that all look the same because drawing is not something I am gifted at.

"Sure. What should I draw?" is what actually comes out of my mouth.

As I push myself out of my chair yet again, my darling daughter scrunches up her face, thinking.

"Let's make a world!" Her face lights up as the brilliant idea comes to her.

"A whole world, huh? Okay, let's draw the world," I reply. "What part of the world should I draw?"

She rummages through the chalk bucket and comes up with a stick of pink chalk and a stick of green. Handing me the green one, she says, "I'll draw the world first. Then we can pick what to put in it."

Bending over and putting her pink chalk to the concrete she begins scooching backward, little by little. She goes up and over the ridge to the flat spot at the top of the drive, then back down the slope, eventually meeting back up to where she started. She has created a bumpy, misshapen circle with some skinny lines and some fat ones and a few gaps here and there. She grabs a purple and a blue from the bucket to fill in the gaps.

"So, what are we going to have in our world?" I ask as she considers which nub of chalk is next. I say "our world" even though it's her imagination doing the work. Sure, it's just chalk on the driveway that's going to wash away in the next rain, but the fact that she's sharing her world with me and asking me to help her create something means a lot.

Without thinking, she rattles off her list. "We need a school and a grocery store and a kitty store. And we need a rainbow and a garden."

"Well, that sounds like a pretty good world. What part should I draw?" I ask, still holding the green chalk.

"I'm going to draw the rainbow and you can draw the school with kids in it," she says. She tries to pick up too many colors at once, clutching them to her scrawny body, and her jacket is suddenly much more colorful than when she put it on. It would have been nice to skip a day of laundry, but playing outside is more important—I can always wash the clothes later.

I crouch down, knees popping, and start drawing a rectangle. I add some windows with the crisscross mullions of every simple house drawing. I add double doors right in the middle and write SCHOOL over the top of the doors. It's challenging to make letters using oversized chalk on an undersized building and a lumpy canvas. What I draw looks roughly like a building with some scribbles on it. I stand up, cocking my head to admire my work. "Eh, pretty good."

She looks up from drawing her rainbow. "But Mom, you forgot the kids. School is for kids, so it needs to have kids." Then she ducks her head back down and tries to squeeze in one more arch. Her rainbow is gray, peach, bright green, and red. Not the colors of a real rainbow and not even very pretty colors together, but it's beautiful in the eyes of a four-year-old.

"Kids. Right," I mutter, peering down at my squiggly rectangle. How do you draw kids *in* a school when you just have the exterior of a school? "How about I draw some kids at recess on a playground?"

"Yeah! There can be some swings and a slide at the playground and kids on them!" she exclaims, running over to stand above my school building to watch the playground materialize. So, I scrunch back down, sitting uncomfortably on the sloping concrete. I start with a stick figure as small as I can with the clumsy medium I'm working with. Then, I add a swing underneath the figure and another next to it. The swing set grows to be half the size of the school. I move on to the slide, complete with a ladder and more stick-kids waiting in line. By the time I have the playground done, it's three times the size of the school. I get to thinking maybe that's the way school should be. More time to play and chitchat in the slide line. More time to swing and admire the funny-colored rainbows of our imagination.

We go on coloring and extending our world. I work on the garden, complete with spiky green grass, a few flowers, and a small tree with tiny red dots on it—apples, I say when she asks why the tree has spots. She draws the kitty store with a green dog and a purple bunny. Nothing we draw is to scale with anything else. We spend the next few minutes admiring our creation and explaining to each other what we drew. This is the best part with little kids. You're not expected to know what they drew when they show it to you; you're expected to ask them questions so they can expand on their creations. If you're lucky, they come up with a pretty good story that rarely has anything to do with what you see. It could appear to be a rock with legs but they'll tell you it's a unicorn on her way to her best friend's house where the friend just discovered a magic door in her closet and they're going on an adventure together to see where the door leads. You only get to hear about the magic door because you asked about the rock.

My husband comes out the front door, taking a break from his work.

"What are you two doing?"

"We made a world, Dad. Can I show you?" My daughter energized by the thought of a new ear to hear about her world.

"Of course you can show me. Tell me about your world," my husband responds, giving me a quick peck on the cheek as he passes.

I walk back to my chair, listening to her going on about all the animals in the kitty store and how it's not just a kitty store, it's just called a kitty store, but really it has all sorts of animals. I'm impressed when she gives me credit for the playground.

"It's not just my world, Dad. Mom and I drew it together, but it's for everyone." There's a brief pause as she admires the work. Then, in true four-year-old fashion, she is done with it. "Do you want to swing with me?" she asks eagerly.

The neighborhood is starting to come alive. The older kids are trickling home from school, the work-from-home neighbors emerge to bask in the early spring sunshine. Some walking dogs, others with earbuds in as they multitask their last call of the day. We wave or exchange small talk as they pass, the main theme being the warmth of the afternoon and the promise of brighter days.

My kid asks for a snack, so my husband disappears inside. My daughter climbs on my lap to wait. She snuggles in, which I love, but it's also uncomfortable. Her bony knees dig into my squishy thighs and her pointy elbows crush what's left of my deformed chest. I wrap her in a hug, kiss her head, and sway gently side to side the way I've been doing every day since she was born. We sit in silence for a minute soaking in the sunshine, and I tell her I love her for the umpteenth time.

Dad comes out the door with apple slices at the same time the neighbor girl heads up our driveway. Her hunger forgotten, my daughter hops off my lap and runs down to meet her friend.

"Mom! Can we do bubbles?" she calls. The girls walk hand in hand up the driveway. My husband goes back into the garage to fish out the bubbles. Our neighbor joins us, and while my daughter describes the world to her friend, we catch up on pleasantries. My husband hands me the bubble tube and I unscrew the wand, waving it back and forth, creating just enough motion to make bubbles. The girls see the bubbles heading in their direction and they shriek with glee. They run in circles, calling to each other, as I dip into the solution again and again, occasionally pitching in to the grown-up conversation on the other side of the driveway.

In our second-story window our cat is sitting on the sill. A bubble floats by and he stands on his back legs trying to swat it through the window with his paw. More bubbles float up and his face bobs as he follows them, trying to figure out how he can get in on the fun. Our grandfather-aged next-door neighbor comes out on his way to an appointment. He stops to chase a few bubbles that make it over to his driveway. Laughing, he looks younger than his years.

More neighbors out for a walk stop to remark on the cheery weather and the sounds of pure joy that can only come from carefree kids under the age of ten.

In this moment, standing on top of our world blowing bubbles, I'm not thinking about cancer, not worried about the future. I'm just here, present. Surrounded by neighbors who have become friends and the cheerful sounds of a spring day, I soak in the sun, the squeals, this beautiful, ordinary moment in time. I take in a breath and let the memory sink in.

As the last of the bubbles float away, the neighbors head home and my husband goes back inside to work. My daughter and I are left on the chalk-covered driveway. She slips her precious little hand into mine as we stand in silence for a minute admiring our world. I hope she's locking away the memory too.

"Mom! Look!" She points to one last lingering bubble wafting over the neighbor's roof as if this moment doesn't want to end, either.

Celestial Haibun
by Mary Camarillo

It's never dark enough in Southern California to see the stars, but I can always find Orion, his seven sirens, knife in sheath, arms and legs splayed to four corners.

Moon rises. Sirens
wail, slice through sleep. Surrender.
Remember to breathe.

Redbird
by Mary Camarillo

Gustavo's mother is now
a hummingbird. He's documented
several surprising visits, sure it is her.

I am sure of nothing.
All I see are her eyes realizing
I would kill her. I keep buying

images of hummingbirds—her urn
has two. The feeder is empty
Dad doesn't want to refill it.

Maybe she's a red bird now
She always liked them—at least
that's what I remember.

Maybe she's a cardinal or a rosy finch
haunting some southern girl
on an Oregon beach.

I picture her more as
as a vermillion flycatcher or scarlet tanager
She always knew how to dress.

but I don't live in those habitats
maybe I never did.

April: A Brief Memoir
by Stephanie Sarver

"April is the cruelest month," at least according to the poet, T. S. Eliot. I first read those words in college long ago. His poem, "The Wasteland," was required reading for English majors. Those words come to mind every April. I've heard them quoted by others, often in response to April downpours and chilly days. Eliot was possibly writing about the aftermath of World War I—scholars still aren't in agreement about his meaning. But he was not writing about April or spring. He also spoke of lilacs breeding from a dead land. The word *breeding* always bothered me. I'm not enough of a poet to forgive his word choice. Horticulturalists may breed plants, but lilacs don't find themselves in April, like rabbits eager to mate, looking for other lilacs with whom to breed. Despite all that, here I am pondering its meaning and reflecting on April.

If I were to agree with Eliot, I might concede that April is cruel especially if we expect more of it by longing for sun or the absence of rain. It is cruel if we expect nature to heed our whining, perhaps justified after many months of the cold, mold-inducing damp of northern Washington where I live. Is April cruel? Or more cruel than February?

When I was young and living at a more southern latitude, April could have figured as a precursor to summer, rather than partial progress toward spring. I never felt disappointed with an April on the Central California coast, or with any season, except perhaps when the summer fogs chilled the beaches. My mother always yearned for sunshine, regarding it a birthright that she never be required to don a raincoat. She attributed her unhappiness to gray skies.

In the California I knew, April was always well into its blooming season. The flowering plum usually bloomed in late January. By April, it was in full leaf. The flowering quince that bloomed pink in February was spent. Camellia blossoms in white and cerise were turning brown, their heavy, fleshy petals accumulating beneath glossy green shrubs. They would continue to bloom into summer. In the Delta, almond orchards were aglow in white, as were the apple orchards of the Pajaro Valley.

One April in the mid-1990s, I travelled from California to Minnesota for a job interview, surprised when I arrived at the sight of dull, brown farm fields rolling endlessly to flat horizons. The trees along the Minnesota River were still bare, the land not yet recovered from its harsh winter.

A year later, I repeated that cycle in reverse, travelling in April from Minnesota to California for a different job interview. In Minnesota, the lilac buds were still closed, the blossoms more of a hint, a promise that wouldn't be fulfilled until May. In my short time there I had grown accustomed to Minnesota, to the long winter that gave way in late March to hints of spring. Across the expanses of neighborhood lawns, the islands of green emerged slowly in the melting snow. I found that even the muted shades of approaching spring were a welcome contrast after months of endless white.

That April, I landed at San Francisco airport and rented a car, driving south to Palo Alto. As I passed through ordinary neighborhoods, I was stunned by bougainvillea and hibiscus in rich bloom, luminescent with magenta and orange, so vivid as to make me squint. I was able to see anew what had once been, to me, ordinary sights. We become inured to the familiar. That was a blessing during my year in Minnesota, immersed in frigid isolation, cloistered at a Lutheran College where I taught for ten months. Until then, I had never understood that winter can endure for six months. I never knew that I could yearn for color.

The April job interview piggybacked on a wedding reception. I felt joyful being home again. I wore a lime-green linen dress, one that certainly would figure as a summer dress in Minnesota. The reception was held outdoors, and the weather was warm enough to be comfortable without even a sweater. The event was memorable only for the dress I wore, and the peculiar conversation I had with a former colleague from business—an engineer. He said I looked like a certain French actress, a woman easily twenty years my senior. He believed that he flattered me or that I'd respond well to such an overture.

I was there in April, because the bride, a former colleague, believed she was doing me a favor in offering me a job, saving me from the career dead-end into which I had fallen after graduate school. I went from professor to administrative assistant, a role that offered a much higher salary. Needing the money, I endured her snipes until she was fired and I was promoted into corporate communications. She later called me, fishing for insider information she could leverage to exercise her stock options. I was chilly. That may have occurred in February, when one could still awaken to an occasional frost.

April figured as the month when the wisteria bloomed. One year, as it bloomed in San Mateo where I lived, it also bloomed in the Castro. The spicy-sweet scent from pendulous purple blossoms lingered in my nostrils, a scent so intense that it's still imprinted on my brain. That scent is paired with a memory of drinking Manhattans at a gay bar, where a couple of patrons loudly observed, "What's *she* doing here?" My date had suggested the place. I sipped my drink as he made meaningful eye contact with the hostile men.

That month a friend, like Eliot's Madame Sosostris, predicted the future for me. "Be wary of this man. He has dark influences." That explained his manner, which confused me, variously attentive and then distant. It wasn't a romance, but a passing acquaintance from graduate school, an entanglement that dissolved, fraught with complications, as quickly as it had formed. Eliot said it well:

Her brain allows one half-formed thought to pass:

"Well now that's done: and I'm glad it's over."

I survived that April, which elided into May. Peace returned and I adorned my apartment deck with impatiens, burnt-orange marigolds, and blue lobelia. The cat found a sunny nook among the flowerpots where she slumbered.

Two years later, April returned as a noteworthy month. My sad brother, living with our enabler mother, faded away entirely. Early April, Mom called to say that something was ailing the brother. I was impatient, unkind. "Of course there's something wrong with him," I said, "He's an alcoholic." She was worried so I drove to Fresno.

April in the San Joaquin Valley was a fine month. The fruit trees were either blooming or coming into leaf. Cotton and alfalfa fields were brilliant greens. I recall the drive to Fresno. Highway 101 to Highway 152 to Highway 99. Take the Clinton Avenue exit near the old Hacienda Hotel. The hotel featured a large neon sign of a Western rider on a rearing horse. History holds that its showroom had boasted dinner shows with Dean Martin and Frank Sinatra. In its heyday, it had three swimming pools.

When I arrived, my brother was incoherent, sprawled on the living room floor. Mom dithered. I could not drag him to the sofa, so I joined him on the floor, embracing and weeping. The next day, I coaxed him to his feet and drove him to the emergency room. The physician, a doctor in training, said, "He is dying." Liver failure. I begged the doctor to admit him. "Don't discharge him to home. My mother can't care for him."

Mercifully, he was granted a private room. I told my sisters, "You need to come now if you want to see him." They visited and he rallied for a week. We laughed at his bedside. The nurse took Polaroid photos. He smiled as we leaned over his bed, our arms enfolding one another. We said our goodbyes and his energy drained away.

The day of the memorial service, already May, was hot. I recited a eulogy, reflecting on the tragedy of addiction. Following the service, I went with my sisters and two of his friends to Playland at Roeding Park to take in the amusement park rides. He would have liked that. We ate Mexican food in a restaurant that featured mariachi music. We were not feeling festive. The adrenaline had faded and we felt only grief. He was gone.

April today. I'm just south of the forty-ninth parallel. That means the sun always hangs low in the sky, though in April it has advanced farther north than in December. In late April, light arrives before 6:00 a.m. and remains until after 8:00 p.m. My California bones still expect sunlight to be accompanied by warmth. But here, the April light is deceptive. Great, gray cumulous clouds still drift across the sun, transforming in a blink the intense warmth of sunshine into a chilling cold.

Trees bloom—red cedar, alder, and ornamental dogwoods—loading the air with pollen. When the clouds pass, the Cascade Range and Mount Baker loom white, buried in snow. Brilliant yellow forsythia joins with the winter heather to respond to the longer days. The daffodils still bloom. Tulips emerge from the cold ground. Grape hyacinth, which blooms in February and March farther south, is in full blossom near the curb in front of my house. Black squirrels dig through flowerpots, foraging for acorns tucked away last fall. Bald eagles dance in pairs in the spring mating ritual that I watch from my office window. Rabbits decimate the gardens as they scamper about, entering into their own spring breeding cycle.

This isn't cruel. It's April.

Skyward
by Marie Eaton

This early morning sky is tender blue
wrapped in a soft fog blanket,

tossed over the islands' shoulders
at the edge of the horizon

Fingers of frost paint crystal patterns
on window glass and over the grass.

And as I watch, sunlight gilds the top branches
of the fir tree, her arms raised in praise

for the morning, every needle and cone
singing hallelujah.

I want to live in praise,
where every moment is a search for joy,

sending my heart skyward like the lark
to sing about the miracle of just this moment.

Ordinary Things
by Marie Eaton

I am in love with ordinary things.
The wooden spoon stirring my soup.

The green teapot on the counter.
My *hori-hori* blade.

The brown chair at the window.
The rosy towel waiting on the bathroom rack.

I love their utility and the way
they always step up to do the job at hand.

I love how the cup holds the tea
or the fork, the bite of salmon.

Like old lovers,
we each know how to do our part.

Distraction
by Marie Eaton

Sometimes I want to be distracted,
pulled sideways by a thread of noticing and wonder.

Chopping carrots for tonight's stew, I look up
and there, across the western sky,

sunset unfurls her crimson scarf
across the horizon.

I drop the knife on the chopping block
and wander out to the deck,

to stand in cool air by the rail and watch
until evening leans over blue islands

to fold sunset's scarf
back into night's pocket.

The Zoo
by Andrea Gabriel
and Janna Jacobson

Welcome to THE ZOO

The world's WILDEST virtual reality dating platform!

"You do you at The Zoo! And you, and you, and you . . ."

8:01 pm EST
Employee ID: GK-Cerberus
Password: GGMSrntyFFS!123

*****

GROUNDSKEEPER CHATTERBOX
#Piazza_San_Marco

Notification: GK-Cerberus has entered the chat

 GK-Assisi

Cerb! Welcome back to your place of gainful employment. After Friday, I thought we'd seen the last of you.

 GK-Cerberus

I thought so too, Assisi. But turns out, I've got rent. OMG. We need Zookeepers, not Groundskeepers. San Marco is packed. You need help?

GK-Assisi

Ugh, it's been nuts. Nothing but noobs. Glad you made it! How'd it go last night? How was the date?

GK-Cerberus

Love is for suckers.

GK-Assisi

And yet, you work at "The world's WILDEST virtual reality dating platform!" Methinks you protest too much.

GK-Cerberus

I repeat. Love is for suckers. Hit me up in dm. I'll give you the gories at break.

GK-Assisi

What the . . . Ahahahaha! Check out Romeo-078756

GK-Cerberus

What's he . . . ?

GK-Assisi

Keeps walking off the edge into the canal. Wanders around underwater, runs into a few walls, then re-rezzes. Rinse and repeat. Time stamp says 20 mins. He's persistent, I'll give him that.

GK-Cerberus

Check his avatar! Is that the cat from the Furry sim?

GK-Assisi

Meeeeow!

GK-Cerberus

Oh wait! Now he's the squid?

GK-Assisi

Yikes! How'd he get access to those avis? San Marco is strictly vanilla.

GK-Cerberus

And now . . . he just broke into a hundred sugar cubes.
Sigh. That's my cue.

GK-Assisi

Sec. I'm pulling his IRL details. Hey, Cerb, go easy on
him "Alan Hawkins, age 72, widowed, retired geology
professor, Bellingham WA."

GK-Cerberus

Oh bless. What's he doing *here*?

GK-Assisi

They gotta stop advertising to the olds. It's just . . . mean.

GK-Cerberus

I got him. BRB?.

*****

**PIAZZA SAN MARCO
IN-SIM CHAT**

Notification: GK-Cerberus has entered Piazza San Marco Sim

GK-Cerberus

Hello. Welcome to The Zoo. I'm Groundskeeper Cer-
berus. Can I help you with anything?

Romeo-078756

. . . H-E-L-L-O . . . I . . . A-M . . . H-A-V-

GK-Cerberus

If you use the voice to text, it's faster

Romeo-078756

. . .

GK-Cerberus

Microphone icon at top left

Romeo-078756

Hello. Ah, that's better! Thank you for helping me!

GK-Cerberus

No problem. It's my job. You seem to be having trouble with your avatar. Can I help?

Romeo-078756

Yes! Thank you. My avatar keeps changing into weird stuff, and I can't make it work right.

GK-Cerberus

What would you *like* your avatar to be?

Romeo-078756

Just, you know, something normal.

GK-Cerberus

How's this?

Romeo-078756

Ha! Not too bad for a romance novel. Where's my shirt?

GK-Cerberus

Better?

Romeo-078756

Hey, hey! Kind of a teenage Cary Grant in a glitter tux look. Heck, *I'd* date me in this getup. Don't you have anything a little more realistic? Or maybe older? There must be a hundred and fifty people in here, and not one of 'em over twenty. How're we supposed to meet people for real when everyone is young and perfect?

GK-Cerberus

It's meant to help users overcome body insecurities, and—

Romeo-078756

If my grandson hadn't bought me this subscription, I'd—

GK-Cerberus

Once you've had a chance to get comfortable, we do have the IRL sim, if you prefer.

Romeo-078756

IRL?

GK-Cerberus

In Real Life. Once you make a Zoo connection, we recommend meeting at the IRL sim before meeting IRL.

Romeo-078756

I'm too old for this.

Notification: Alice has entered Piazza San Marco Sim

Alice

Hello. Are you a groundskeeper?

GK-Cerberus

I am. Welcome, Alice. Is this your first time in the Zoo?

Alice

No, but I *am* new. Is it that obvious?

GK-Cerberus

Only because Piazza San Marco is the first sim, where we get everyone oriented. Nice choice on your avi. I bet half our users don't even know who Marilyn Monroe is!

Alice

Thank you. I'm learning. But I can't figure out how to get to the other sims. Can you help me?

GK-Cerberus

Not a problem. There's a menu on the bottom left of your screen with sim choices. Or from here, you can just hop a boat in one of the canals.

*****

GROUNDSKEEPER CHATTERBOX
#Piazza_San_Marco

GK-Assisi

Cerb! Check Alice's IRL! 70 yo retired librarian, Bellingham WA!

GK-Cerberus

No way

GK-Assisi

Way! And her Zoo Match with Romeo is 100%! 100% *never* happens! It's meant to be, Cerb. You gotta help 'em out.

GK-Cerberus

What's going on? Did corporate drop 2-for-1 coupons at the senior center?

GK-Assisi

Actually, they kinda did. They're trying out a new age/location AI group algorithm.

GK-Cerberus

OMG. Kill me now.

GK-Assisi

Aww. I think it's sweet.

GK-Cerberus

Love is violent. We gotta protect the olds.

GK-Assisi

How'd you get so jaded?

GK-Cerberus

It's a short, sad story.

GK-Assisi

Grab a drink with me after work. Tell me the whole thing.

GK-Cerberus

. . .

GK-Assisi

Sorry, didn't mean to—

GK-Cerberus

No, it's okay, just surprised, and—

GK-Assisi

Uh oh! Romeo needs you.

GK-Cerberus

Oh jeez. How'd he turn himself upside down? Maybe some Hide and Seek will be fun for them?

GK-Assisi

Don't you dare!

GK-Cerberus

Out of the frying pan and—

GK-Assisi

Oooh! You nasty.

GK-Cerberus

Heh heh.

*****

**PIAZZA SAN MARCO
IN-SIM CHAT**

Romeo-078756

Hello

A **Alice**

Hello. Nice tuxedo.

Notification: Pansexxx Panthser has entered Piazza San Marco Sim

R **Romeo-078756**

I'm just glad I don't have horns. Nice to meet you. I've got a neighbor named Alice. I like that name.

Notification: Aphrodite Sparklebutz has entered Piazza San Marco Sim

R **Romeo-078756**

Did I mention that Alice is a nice name?

A **Alice**

Thank you. And are you really named Romeo?

R **Romeo-078756**

I'm Alan. I couldn't figure out the name thingy.

A **Alice**

That's funny. I have a neighbor named Alan too.

R **Romeo-078756**

What are the odds that—

🐾 **GK-Cerberus**

If you two want to follow me, I can take you to your first real sim.

A **Alice**

I'm game if you are, Alan

R **Romeo-078756**

I've got a bad feeling about this, but why not? After you, Ms. Monroe.

*****

MERMAID GROTTO
IN-SIM CHAT

Notification: GK-Cerberus has entered Mermaid Grotto Sim
Notification: Alice has entered Mermaid Grotto Sim
Notification: Romeo-078756 has entered Mermaid Grotto Sim

A   **Alice**

Ooh! This is pretty! Look at the jewels in the walls! And pirate's treasure!

R   **Romeo-078756**

Hey! I've got a cutlass. And a patch. That's fun. Ahoy there, lassie!

🐕   **GK-Cerberus**

Mermaid Grotto *is* one of the faves, and—

A   **Alice**

Look! In the pool! Real mermaids!

R   **Romeo-078756**

Look at yourself. You've got a fish tail. HaHA!

A   **Alice**

Guess that's better than horns, eh Alan?

🐕   **GK-Cerberus**

So, I've set the sims to Hide and Seek mode. The way this works is—

A   **Alice**

Can I swim with it?

R   **Romeo-078756**

Give it a go!

🐕   **GK-Cerberus**

If I could get your attention for just a min—

A | **Alice**

I can't walk with a tail.

R | **Romeo-078756**

Here. I'll carry you.

A | **Alice**

Hahaha! Oh my! How dashing, I—

A | **Alice**

OOOoooooooOOOOOoooooooOOOOooooooo

R | **Romeo-078756**

What happened to her?

GK-Cerberus

Mermaid singing. You'll have to jump in to understand her. But before you go, you should know that Hide and Seek mode will change your sim at random, and you might want to set your—

R | **Romeo-078756**

Wait for me, Alice! I'm coming!

GK-Cerberus

…maturity settings.

R | **Romeo-078756**

OOOoooooooOOOOOoooooooOOOOooooooo

*****

GROUNDSKEEPER CHATTERBOX
#Private_Chat

GK-Assisi

You'll probably go to hell for that.

GK-Cerberus

I didn't think they'd go feral on me!

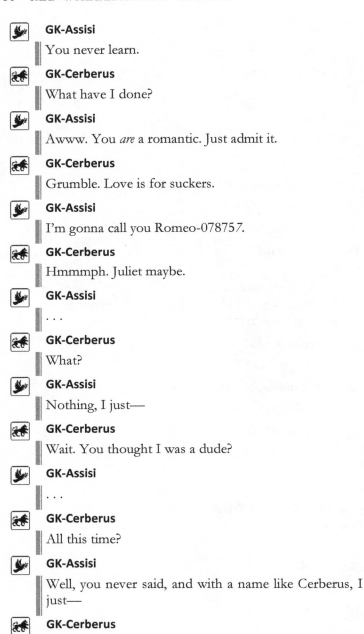

GK-Assisi

You never learn.

GK-Cerberus

What have I done?

GK-Assisi

Awww. You *are* a romantic. Just admit it.

GK-Cerberus

Grumble. Love is for suckers.

GK-Assisi

I'm gonna call you Romeo-078757.

GK-Cerberus

Hmmmph. Juliet maybe.

GK-Assisi

. . .

GK-Cerberus

What?

GK-Assisi

Nothing, I just—

GK-Cerberus

Wait. You thought I was a dude?

GK-Assisi

. . .

GK-Cerberus

All this time?

GK-Assisi

Well, you never said, and with a name like Cerberus, I just—

GK-Cerberus

OMG! I gotta go.

*****

GROUNDSKEEPER CHATTERBOX
#Private_Chat

GK-Assisi

911!

GK-Skick

Whaddup, my dude?

GK-Assisi

Did you know Cerb is a she/her?

GK-Skick

Wait, what?

GK-Assisi

Cerb is a FEMALE PERSON!

GK-Skick

No

GK-Assisi

Dying

GK-Skick

Hahahahaha! All the times you're like, "if only Cerb were a girl, I'd be in love!" Hahahahaha!

GK-Assisi

All the times I tried to get him . . . er, her . . . into IRL after hours, just to grab a beer. Ugh, she must think . . .

GK-Skick

Sec. I'm checking your Zoo Match Rating.

GK-Assisi

Dude, no!

GK-Skick

. . .

GK-Assisi

What's it say?

GK-Skick

100%

GK-Assisi

I think I'm gonna be sick

*****

AERIAL CASCADES
IN-SIM CHAT

Notification: Alice has entered Aerial Cascades Sim
Notification: Romeo-078756 has entered Aerial Cascades Sim

Romeo-078756

Argh! Take that, you scurvy dog! Why I oughtta . . . wait.
Where are we? Where's my cutlass?

Alice

Oh no. My tail is gone. Where are we, Alan?

Romeo-078756

What is this place?

Alice

Oh God. I'm afraid of heights.

Romeo-078756

I'm not, and even *I* feel a little sick. Nothing but floating
pools and waterfalls as far as I can see.

Alice

I can't look! How far down does it go?

Romeo-078756

I can't see the bottom. Just more sky.

[A] **Alice**

> I'll see if I can call that Cerberus person to get us out of here. I'll just—

[R] **Romeo-078756**

> Alice, no!

Notification: Alice has left Aerial Cascades Sim

*****

RED LIGHT AMSTER-DAYAM!
IN-SIM CHAT

Notification: Romeo-078756 has entered Red Light Amster-Dayam! Sim

[R] **Romeo-078756**

> Aliiiiiice! Alice, are you here? Oh! Excuse me.

[😫] **Salty Longstaff**

> Hi there! I can be Alice, Daddy.

[R] **Romeo-078756**

> Erm. Ah, sorry, I think I'm in the wrong—

[😫] **Salty Longstaff**

> Oh settle down, Romeo. I won't bite . . . not unless you ask . . .

Notification: GK-Cerberus has entered Red Light Amster-Dayam! Sim
Notification: GK-Assisi has entered Red Light Amster-Dayam! Sim

[🐕] **GK-Cerberus**

> Hey Romeo, how's it going?

[R] **Romeo-078756**

> What happened to Alice? I can't find her.

GK-Cerberus

She's here somewhere. I can see her in the dash.

 Romeo-078756

Along with a thousand other people! How will I find her again? And . . . oh my word. What is happening on the dance floor?

 Salty Longstaff

New dance called The Centipede.

Notification: Salty Longstaff has offered the object Penis v2.0 to Romeo-078756

 Romeo-078756

Aghh! What the—What is that thing?

 Salty Longstaff

Your avi, love. I checked the specs. It's not anatomically correct.

 Romeo-078756

Look, Mr. Longstaff, I'm sure you mean well, but I'm looking for my friend, and—

 Salty Longstaff

Click the X in the menu box.

Notification: Romeo-078756 has accepted the object Penis v2.0 from Salty Longstaff

 Romeo-078756

No! I don't want—

 GK-Cerberus

Actually, you should take it. It's a generous gift. In some of the sims you'll need—

R **Romeo-078756**

I don't want any of that! I just want to find Alice! I didn't get her phone number.

🕊 **GK-Assisi**

Hey! Look who I found over in the Kitty Kat Lounge.

🐾 **GK-Cerberus**

Alice! Thank goodness. Romeo here was worried.

A **Alice**

Alan? Is that you? I'm so glad I found you! I was just talking to a contortionist named Aimlow Godeep. But then GK-Assisi here found me and brought me to you.

R **Romeo-078756**

Alice! I thought I'd lost you!

Notification: Romeo-078756 has dropped the object Penis v2.0, and it has been returned by the property owner at Red Light Amster-Dayam

R **Romeo-078756**

Er. I can explain that.

A **Alice**

Alan, I really liked meeting you, but I don't know if this place is for me, to be honest.

R **Romeo-078756**

Wanna blow this popsicle stand?

🐾 **GK-Cerberus**

If you like, I can pop you both into the IRL sim. Still a sim, but with your real faces.

A **Alice**

Oh . . . I don't know. I mean . . . I look nothing like Marilyn, and—

☐R☐ **Romeo-078756**

> Well, I sure as hell don't look like Cary Grant in a glitter
> tux. C'mon. What've we got to lose?

*****

IRL COFFEE SHOP
IN-SIM CHAT

Notification: Romeo-078756 has entered IRL Coffee Shop Sim
Notification: Alice has entered IRL Coffee Shop Sim

☐A☐ **Alice**

> . . .

☐R☐ **Romeo-078756**

> You look awfully familiar.

☐A☐ **Alice**

> Alan? Is that you? Alan from next door?

☐R☐ **Romeo-078756**

> Wait a minute! You're Alice Watson? *My* Alice Watson?

☐A☐ **Alice**

> I'm just . . . oh my goodness, how embarrassing.

☐R☐ **Romeo-078756**

> Embarrassing? Why? I've been wanting to invite you out
> for years!

☐A☐ **Alice**

> You're just being gallant.

☐R☐ **Romeo-078756**

> Not at all. In fact, if you're willing, let's get out of here.
> I've got a perfectly good pot of coffee in my very own
> IN REAL LIFE kitchen.

A **Alice**

I can't think of anything better!

R **Romeo-078756**

Meet you there?

A **Alice**

You've got it, Romeo!

*****

GROUNDSKEEPER CHATTERBOX
#IRL_Coffee_Shop

GK-Assisi

C'mon. You've gotta admit that was sweet.

GK-Cerberus

Grumble. Maybe

GK-Assisi

Meet me IRL to discuss? Get a drink maybe?

GK-Cerberus

. . .

GK-Assisi

?

GK-Cerberus

You know? Why not? Lead the way, Romeo.

On the Day after the Naming of the Buddhas
by Maureen Kane

On the Day after the Naming of the Buddhas
The Empress returned home and unbound her hair,
letting it fall in cascades.

She unnamed them all.

Brushing her hair
she shed Siddhārtha
and Gautama.
Vipaśyin came out in a knot.
Viśvabhū and Śikhin tangled together
and tried to stay.
She coaxed them apart
and swept them away.

Nārada said, "I love you and I understand,"
as he willingly slid from her crown.

Sujāta tried to hide behind her ear,
but she asked him to leave as well.

Stepping over the snarls and tangles on the floor,
she lowered herself into a fragrant bath
of river water and rose oils.

Miracle Hunter
by Maureen Kane

When the recycling truck took away the tub rejected last week I thought, *Well, that was a miracle. What if today I became a miracle hunter?*

I began the day looking for water transmuting into wine, and cancer cures, but found something else. Everything sparkled.

The blue hydrangeas sang through their blossoming, *Here we are, bigger than ever, take up space and breathe, it's glorious.* Fresh garlic pulled from the garden freely offered the ecstasy of its spicy, loamy essence. The salad shared twelve hues of green and even a bit of purple, some leaves with red stalks. Each tasting a little different. One like lemon pepper!

And people. Walking by people I don't know brought a special joy. Every one a miracle of others meeting a generation ago at the right time. Each life, a new novel to explore and be moved by. I saw a woman painting a lake and mountains. Her mountains were pink, and the lake green. The miracle of disobeying rules for beauty. I wish I'd stopped to get to know her.

Later, my husband called from 3,745 miles away and we could talk. Me in bed, and he eating lunch. That same phone connected me to my aging mother, and today I had the patience and the right words to deepen the conversation.

I think my new medicine will be consuming three miracles a day.

Toll: A Fantastic Kind of Crazy
by Anneliese Kamola

I wrestled my hiking backpack between my train seat and the one in front of me, so I could keep access to the top pouch. Straddling my pack, I slipped into the window seat, and as the train lugged from the station, opened the top pouch and pulled out computer paper, a needle, thread, glue stick, and pair of scissors. With almost five hours between Munich and Freiburg im Breisgau, I could use the time and save a few dollars making my own book.

I had already filled two journals with frantic scribbling about my time in Berlin, Munich, the Dachau Concentration Camp, and other places from my family history. Unlike so many of the people in their twenties I had met in hostels, this post-college trip for me was not about letting loose. I wished I could relax like my peers. But partying in loud clubs with bright lights and cigarette smoke, getting drunk on dark German beer, or touring castles did not fulfill me. I was on a pilgrimage to understand the root of emotional pain in my relationship with my dad.

I had grown up in fear of Dad's emotional explosions. On any given day, he would go from even-tempered to blowing up at me for accidentally tracking mud into the front entryway or for not vacuuming the orange rug in the family room by the time I had said I would. Some nights after coming home from work he stormed through the house, slamming cupboard doors and chewing me out for leaving anything as much as a paper out of place.

Yet as much as I resented him for causing me emotional harm, I held a depth of compassion that surprised even me—because I knew rage too. Wildfires of emotion also razed my body, driving me to say and do things I did not mean to do. Once I slammed an apple core against my friend's head, shame descending only when I saw the shock and pain contorting her face. The blinding power of my anger—and what I was capable of—terrified me.

And I saw Dad struggle too. I watched as he lost his temper with his father, my Opa, and felt how their ricocheting fury seemed so like my own. And I heard the bitterness in Opa's voice the one time he mentioned his mother's strict control and how she ruled the house "with an iron spine." I longed to understand all of the reasons our family line lived with this force that was larger than any of us. If I could understand it, I could understand myself too.

So many friends had told me before I left how adventure awaited, how I would easily make friends, and to stay open to the magic of spontaneous plans. I had been encouraged to trust and follow my feet. But traveling solo, across an ocean and on another continent and without anyone who understood me, my anger retreated, and loneliness filled the space. Isolation became almost-paralyzing indecisiveness. Which of this city's six hostels should I stay at? Which sandwich should I buy? Bus or train? Stand in line for a museum and pay money for admittance or walk around the city as a window-tourist for free?

The night before, I had slept poorly, not only from a lumpy mattress and thin pillow, but after repeated awakenings by late-night partiers returning to the hostel. When I finally hauled myself down the stairs to the dining area for breakfast, I sat alone, forcing myself to eat plain muesli with milk—the cheapest of hostel breakfast options. The loneliness felt heavy. I was too serious. I wasn't any fun. I had no friends, and I felt crazy for embarking on this journey. Even after almost a month of traveling I still did not understand who I was or how to get out of the endless maze of painful emotions. My backpack and journals were, thus far, my only travel companions.

As the train picked up speed, an elderly woman walked slowly from the door toward the seats, regal even amidst the rocking of the moving train. She sat in a backward-facing seat across the aisle from me. Her wrinkles framed elegant features, and she had tied her white hair into a knot on the top of her head. A thick green-and-blue-plaid shawl draped over her shoulders, covering a simple gray dress. Sensible pumps adorned her knobby feet.

Feeling shy, I looked out the window to watch the forest flick by before turning back to my journal-making. I began folding groups of four sheets of paper in half, making twelve folded bundles in all. I had taken the pages from the hostel's recycling bin that morning—they were mostly blank. As the forests gave way to farmlands, I used an unthreaded needle to puncture holes through the center folds of each bundle, the repetitive motion soothing my travel anxieties.

The sounds of quiet conversations in German were far from harsh to my ears. They sounded like water over stones in an alpine creek, and for a moment I missed the summer mountain hikes of the Pacific Northwest. The train hugged a forest on the right side of the tracks, replanted trees growing in rows, not like the wild woods of Washington State. On the left side, strikingly yellow fields of *Brassica rapa*—or *Raps* as the plant was known in German—undulated. The blossoms seemed to hold sunshine in tangible form. One day the seeds would be pressed into canola oil.

The train conductor entered the car and approached the elderly woman to check her ticket. I put down my project in the empty seat beside me and retrieved my ticket from my old journal, tucked in the front pouch of my pack. The conductor crossed the aisle toward me, looking official in her navy-blue uniform, and I handed her my ticket. She scanned the barcode with her handheld machine, said something in German, returned the ticket, and moved on to the passenger behind me.

After sliding my ticket into my used journal, which I slipped into the seat pocket in front of me, I threaded the needle and pulled the string through the first bundle of paper. Glancing across the aisle, I saw the elderly woman watching me. I aligned the holes with a second bundle of folded papers, then stitched up and through in a crisscross pattern. Then I tugged the thread tight, so the bundles of paper snugged together—just as I longed to pull myself closer to understanding my lineage.

I had learned to make hand-bound books in college from my favorite English professor, Mary Cornish, who also taught me how to write like a musician—paying attention to the sound and rhythm of words. She taught us how to make hand-bound books so we could write our truth in a space that was completely, *completely*, our own.

After sewing twelve bundles together into the body of a book, I pulled two unused postcards from my old journal, one a painted image of a mountain and the other a black-and-white image of a woman's face. I had purchased both in the Munich train station. I uncapped a glue stick and glued the postcards to the first and last pages of the journal, creating front and back covers. When I was done, I held an almost-six inch by just-over-eight-inch journal.

I continued to observe the woman through brief side-glances. She wore makeup, but not too much. Her hands rested on the handle of her cane, and her skin looked soft. A cross pendant on a silver chain rested prominently on her chest.

I sensed her kindness. The woman's attention reminded me of how my Oma, my German grandmother, watched while I worked on craft projects as a small child.

As the train curved around a corner, squares of yellow fields alternated with fields of chartreuse barley and brown, fallow soil. I slid the needle onto the spool's thread, then wrapped the end of the thread around both the needle and spool a few times for security. I capped the glue and tucked it, the scissors, and the needle and thread into the top pouch of my pack, exchanging them for a pen. As I sat up, poised to write, I heard the woman say something in German.

I looked at her directly and shook my head.

"Sorry," I said. "I don't know what you are saying. *Sprechts du* English?"

I had learned many people in Germany spoke English, so it was not an unreasonable request.

"This is beautiful, what you make," she replied, before patting the blue upholstered seat next to her. I looked at the homemade journal. Beautiful? I tucked my pen next to my old journal in the seat pocket, then stood and shimmied around my belongings. I crossed the aisle, bracing against the train's rocking, and handed her the newly created journal as I sat.

"*Sehr Schoen,*" she said, turning it over in her hands. "Very beautiful. Where do you journey from?" Her voice sounded like velvet.

"Um. The United States. Near Seattle."

She looked at me in earnest. "So far from home."

"Are you traveling by yourself too?" I asked.

"*Ja.* But just from my home to my daughter's. I do not go far anymore." She paused, looking at me. "*Schreibst du?*" she asked, mimicking the motion of writing.

"Yes, I write. Every day. What I feel, what I wish to know about my family, the good and the bad things I'm learning about myself while I'm traveling." I shrugged. "My loneliness and fears, and how I don't feel like a normal twenty-two-year-old. I have already filled two journals, so I made a third."

Why was I telling her all of this? I hadn't felt comfortable talking with anyone for days, and yet here I was spilling my tender truths. She held me in her steady gaze. I felt comforted, almost as if she had given me a long-wanted hug.

"*Du bist toll,*" she finally stated.

"*Was ist 'toll'?*" I replied. In asking for the definition of the word "toll," I had not realized I had spoken an entire German sentence.

The woman made an "mmm" sound through her closed mouth. She set my journal on her lap and, instead of answering me with words, adjusted her body—clenching her fists, bringing her elbows in close to her sides, sitting up straight, shoulders back, eyes level. She took a deep breath. Her body said: Resolute. Grounded. Courageous.

"Ah. *Toll.* I understand that. Yes. I . . ." I paused. "I suppose I am." I didn't fully believe myself, even as I said it.

"And you travel by yourself?" she asked.

I nodded.

"You travel by yourself. From the other side of the world. *Woa.* You are strong. Power!"

I felt anything but powerful. But her eyes glittered, and she pointed her finger gently toward me.

"I traveled many years by myself when I was young, like you. I liked it. People thought I was crazy." She shook her head and smiled, remembering, turning my journal over between her hands again. Then she bobbed her head left and right. "*Ja*, maybe so. Maybe crazy. But the good kind of crazy. This is what *toll* means—a fantastic crazy. You know?" She looked at me.

Somehow her enthusiasm soothed my exhaustion and reminded me of why I was on the train—following a thirst to find an answer to my family legacy. I could feel my energy within, bright and alive. Urgent and real.

"Some people don't get it," she continued, looking around at the other people in the car as if to show how common it was to not understand.

"No," I said, thinking of Dad, and the party-travelers I had met. "Some people don't understand this kind of solo travel."

"*Ja*. It is something one must *do* to understand," she said.

"Did you feel scared when you traveled for a long time by yourself?" I asked her.

She looked at me and nodded. "Yes, of course. It is part of facing yourself. You must take off everything you think you know, and then choose to put back on what you want. It hurts. To do this by *choice* is the crazy part."

She was making a new kind of sense. I had thought my discomfort was about not knowing how to navigate the physical world, but perhaps it had more to do with surrendering control.

"Is it hard for you?" she asked.

I nodded, finally admitting my vulnerability to someone other than myself.

I hadn't liked who I had been while traveling. Hesitant. Afraid. Even suspicious. A week before I had blown up at a total stranger in a hostel because he offered me a beer. I didn't know why I had yelled, all I knew afterwards was that I didn't want to lead with a short fuse anymore—with my father, or friends, or strangers. But changing that pattern required looking directly into my rage.

"Yes, I don't always feel like it's a good idea to travel. I second-guess myself a lot. What am I doing out here, on the other side of the world? Am I nuts?" I shook my head.

"*Ja*," she smiled, seeming to be proud of me. "*Fantastisch*. You are *toll*. You have what it takes."

I stared at her, how she crossed her ankles and sat patiently. Something in the stillness of that moment lit a fire in my belly— a kind of heat that was not a roar but a quiet tending. Was travel-ing by myself teaching me the strength I needed to face my power? Could I find the courage to face hard truths about my actions and take responsibility for all that seemed uncontrollable within me? In the presence of her calm, I could sense the version of myself I wanted to become: a woman who had endured the discomfort of unknown worlds—physical and emotional—to find equanimity. A woman who had changed her family's pattern.

An automated announcement rumbled over the train's inter-com, and the woman handed my journal back to me.

"*Aso*, I get off here."

I held the book between my palms, feeling the warmth from her hands lingering on the smooth covers. I imagined her kind-ness infusing the pages on which I was destined to write, perhaps guiding my pen to deeper discoveries.

The woman picked up her purse from the seat facing us before turning toward me again. She grew very still then leaned toward me, staring right into my eyes.

"Power! You *must* go by yourself. You are strong—do not doubt yourself. Whatever you are facing, it is *necessary* for you to grow."

The train began to slow, and she stood. Holding my journal with my right hand, I also stood and stepped backward into the aisle to let her pass. She leaned against her cane and took my left hand in her free one. Her wrinkles framed the faintest smile tugging at the corners of her cheeks. She said quietly, *"Du bist ein toll Frauen.* Do not forget this."

I couldn't help the tears that misted my eyes. *"Und du bist ein toll Oma."* I tried to pack a million thank-yous into the moment.

I wished we had more time together. I could have curled up on the seat next to her and listened to stories for hours. I longed to know her name and the details of her life, where she had traveled, the characters she had met. What did she know of furor, and how did she manage her fear? I wanted to ask about her conviction, and how, exactly, she had built such a sense of peace.

Instead, I nodded. She dropped my hand, turned, and walked with surprising balance down the gently rocking train towards the exit door.

I curled back into my seat and retrieved my pen as a dozen passengers rose and headed to the front of the car. The train stopped at the station and I heard the doors hiss open. From my window I watched the elderly woman descend the stairs step-by-step, slowly cross the platform amidst a rushing crowd, and disappear down the escalator.

I held my journal in my hands, feeling her confidence in me. She was right—the time and courage devoted to learning my story was precious. It was okay not to party like the others my age, but to let an organic shedding of identity happen, and be courageous enough to allow vulnerability to crack me open. Perhaps in that new space, I might find a still-unknown panacea for my family pain and return home with a sense of ancestral reconciliation.

As the train started up again, increasing speed until it whipped through the rolling green hills of my ancestors, the woman's words echoed in my memory—*Power! You must go by yourself. You are strong.* Power was not just rage and self-protection. Power was also the courage to change. I didn't know exactly how, but I promised myself that someday I would model a new kind of *toll* to future generations. I opened my journal and began to write.

Unrivaled
by Deidra Suwanee Dees

Muscogee pearls
unrivaled by

diamond or jewel

thin strand,

loose end waving

from the magnolia leaf,

clear water droplets
in beaded
succession

line up on the spider's strand
as dew

retreats from first light.

Strong Muscogee Womxn
by Deidra Suwanee Dees

I am a strong Muscogee womxn
    carrying my children with me
        as I walk into my future

  I am a strong Muscogee womxn
      carrying my children with me
          as I walk into my future

    I am a strong Muscogee womxn
        carrying my children with me
            as I walk into my future

      I am a strong Muscogee womxn
          carrying my children with me
              as I walk into my future

Scent of Cedar
by Deidra Suwanee Dees

shu-shu-shu-shu—shu-shu-shu-shu

shu-shu-shu-shu—shu-shu-shu-shu,

turtle shell shakers,

ancestral chants,

scent of cedar in my hair

call my toddler to dance beside me

The Beginner
by Seán Dwyer

Many boys and girls enjoy summer camp, and I was one of them. I attended Camp Goodfellow, a green space near Lake Michigan. It's unfortunate that a percentage of the kids found camp to be an escape, rather than just an escapade. I was one of them.

The summer I turned nine, I attended camp, even though my mom was in the hospital. I see now that one goal was to give my dad respite while he tended to Mom. The next year, Mom was dead, and camp was one of four places I stayed that summer.

My age-eleven camp experience was, I now realize, a life-saving dot on my timeline. When Dad and his new girlfriend dropped me off on Sunday, Dad said to have fun.

His girlfriend, though, asked, "Are you going to learn to swim this year? You can't stay afraid of the water your whole life."

I said I would try.

The pool was half the size of an Olympic pool, with a low-slung diving board at the deep end. On Sunday afternoon, the swimming instructor lined up all the boys and tested our skills, a precursor to Harry Potter's Sorting Hat.

I wasn't good at sports, but there was a difference between being lousy at basketball and not being able to swim. A basketball couldn't kill you, and I didn't fear the sport. But I had almost drowned during a swimming lesson at Cedar Lake when I was seven, and after that, I was done with water. When I was nine, I spent my week of swimming classes standing upright in the pool. I refused to put my head underwater. I knew I couldn't see or hear underwater, and in such a grim place as a pool, I wanted control of all five senses.

Now it was my third year of camp, and I was eleven, which made me a veteran. It was only an hour after the family dropped me off that the call came to assemble for swimming tests. I joined the other boys, last names A through M, at the fence to the pool. The Advanced and Intermediate swimmers tested and went to play. Then I shed my sneakers and waded in sanitizing bleach water, which was about as deep as I really wanted to go. Several boys and I formed a semicircle around the pool. The counselor climbed out of the water.

My stomach knotted when I saw her.

"Hi, guys. I'm Beverly. Some of you can swim a little bit, so you'll be the Advanced Beginners. If you can float or get partway across the pool, hop on in."

I watched Beverly work with the Advanced Beginners. Soon they left, and it was down to me, seven other pale, skinny boys, and a tall twelve-year-old named Drago.

"Okay, guys, let's give it a try," she said, almost in a whisper. She shook her damp, honey-brown hair off her shoulders. I fixed her with an owl-like stare. "So, you guys aren't much for swimming. How many of you have been to Goodfellow Camp before?"

Five boys raised their hand, including me. I recognized Drago and Brian, the latter being a very white boy with dark hair who had chucked up his first camp lunch in the pool two years ago. That was the only time I moved quickly in the water without fear of going under. Back then, Sean Glancy, my cabin mate for the past two years, was a Beginner. Now he was an Intermediate, and I was more alone at the pool than ever.

Beverly continued, "If you were Beginners last year, maybe you need some extra help to get used to the water. I'll try to make it easy and not scary this week, okay?"

Everyone else nodded. I just stared.

"Who wants to be the first to see it's not so bad?" I realized my mouth was open, and I tried to close it. Beverly looked at me. "How about you?"

I had removed my glasses, so I was not completely sure she was looking at me, but she beckoned in my direction. I looked to either side.

"Yes, you, sir, if that's okay." I nodded quickly and stepped slowly toward her through the warm water. A rush of chlorine hit my nostrils.

I looked down. Sunlight glinted off crisscrossed surface ripples like diamonds, and it traced white streaks like short flashes of lightning on the powder-blue floor of the pool. When I saw Beverly's toes, I looked up again.

She pulled back her hair again with a smooth gesture of her hand. Her hair smelled of strawberries. Her hazel eyes smiled at me. I saw her high cheekbones, her slender nose, her full lips, and delicate chin.

"What's your name?"

"Seán Dwyer, ma'am."

She smiled. "Call me Beverly."

Beverly.

"Okay, Seán. Now, give me your hands." My *hands?* "I won't let you fall." *That was not the problem.* "Go ahead, Seán." I held out my hands, and she grasped them. Her grip was firm, warm, and steady, unlike my shaky hands.

"Okay, I'm going to drop down partway in the water, and you do it with me. Up to your mouth, but not your nose. Okay?"

I braced myself. Up close I could see more details of Beverly. Perfect eyebrows, perfect teeth. A scattering of brown freckles. She wore a medium-blue bikini.

Beverly started to bend her knees and I followed suit. As the water climbed up her abdomen, I saw her flat stomach grow pale beneath the surface. Her navel was tiny, and her hips broadened smoothly into her bikini bottom. In a few moments, we were knee to knee, eye to eye. The water had made us the same height.

"Okay, Seán, blow bubbles for me." She pursed her lips and blew toward me, and I blew back.

"Now with your nose." Helpless to say no to her, I lowered my face a bit to match hers, and I blew bubbles through my nose. She winked at me, and I almost sucked in a lungful of water.

"Good work, Seán. We'll have you swimming yet." She stood, and I followed slowly. She turned to the other boys, and I saw the curve of her buttocks under her bikini. I shook my head to clear it, and some water from my hair landed on her arm. She looked back at me, chuckled, and flicked some water at me with her fingertips. Her nails were painted the same blue as her bikini.

Comfortable in my sleeping bag that night after "Taps," I turned on my side and moved my pillow, but I couldn't sleep. I listened to the crickets and tried to blank my mind. She would not go away. Beverly in the water, holding my hands; Beverly climbing out of the pool, dripping water as if she were in the shower; Beverly smelling of strawberries and something minty on the breath she blew into my face.

Beginning with Monday breakfast, I sat where I could steal glances of Beverly at our meals. If I had just this week, I had to memorize her, soak her up. I could keep her in my heart forever if I worked at it.

I had my first class of Athletics with Steve, a tall, raw-boned, blond guy with wildly curly hair. Steve's thing was softball, and that was fine with me. The Nature teacher was Malcolm, the first man I had ever met who tried to look like John Lennon.

After Nature was Swimming. I ran back to the cabin and changed quickly, then rushed across the lawn to the pool so I could watch Beverly swim. She waved to me, and I sat on a bench near the fence and watched as she dove into the water and swam two lengths with smooth, efficient strokes. She scooped herself onto the concrete and walked over to me.

"Ready to go, Seán?" *She still knew my name.*

"Yes. This year I want to learn to swim."

She looked into my eyes. "It's not as bad as you probably think. Do you know why you don't like it?"

I told her about Cedar Lake. She nodded as I talked.

"Well, you can't see underwater in Cedar Lake, but you can in the pool. You can hear, too. Almost as well as when you're above water. And I'll be around to keep anything from happening to you, okay?" The corner of her mouth rose in a half-grin.

I nodded.

"Great." She ruffled my hair and stood. "If you come early, we can talk whenever you want to."

I couldn't stand. My knees had turned to water. The other Beginners were wandering out of the bath house, not nearly as eagerly as I had. They all climbed into the pool behind me, hesitating and grimacing.

"Okay, guys, today we are going to try to get you used to the idea of getting your face wet. How many of you hate that?" I counted six hands. I kept mine down.

"I need someone to get this started." She looked at me, and I raised my hand a bit.

"Good, Seán. Come here." I sloshed over to where she was standing, five feet from the side of the pool, outside my comfort zone.

"I didn't want to put you on the spot by picking you, but I thought you would be the best example," she said quietly. I felt my face burn. She turned to the other boys.

"I'm going to show Seán how to get used to having his face in the water. I'll have all of you try this. I'll get some water in my hands, and Seán will stick his face in the water and blow. You guys can keep your eyes closed when you make bubbles if you want to."

She cupped some water in her hands, and I saw her slender fingers, distorted by the water, waiting to cradle my face. I leaned forward, fighting the urge to pull back. I took a deep breath and nestled my chin against her comforting fingertips. The crown of my head brushed against her belly.

I blew into the water. When my breath was halfway gone, I pushed my lips against her fingers and kissed them. She didn't flinch, so I hoped she thought it was just part of the breathing.

"Good!" she said when I ran out of air. I looked up; her breasts framed her smile. I stepped back and looked away. I felt the sun on my neck. A light breeze toyed with her hair.

"Who's next?" The rest of the boys came grudgingly, and some of them could not get their face into her hands. I wondered how they could pass up such an opportunity.

That evening, Sean Glancy and I were in the cabin when a truck came around to fog the grounds with DDT. We climbed up on the shelving above the cots and tried to avoid breathing the smelly fog, pretending it was a poison gas we had to flee.

While we were waiting for the air to clear, Sean said, "I wish you were an Intermediate swimmer. Then we could be in all the same classes."

"Next year I will be. I'm going to learn to swim this year."

Sean's eyes widened. "You think so? Wow. That would be cool. I didn't think any Beginner ever learned to swim."

"I'll be the first."

As Lights Out approached, I went to the central bathroom to rinse my face. I looked around; no one was in there. Quickly I plugged a sink and filled it with water. I stuck my face in it and started blowing, my eyes squeezed shut.

I heard footsteps. I started scrubbing my face, rinsing it from the sink. Drago peeked in on me.

"Man, you really aren't scared of water now," he said. "I wish you'd tell me your secret."

I wiped my face on my shirt. "I just decided water was okay. If you just believe, you can do it too, Drago."

"I'll try. Good night."

The week rolled on. Beverly held my hands as I placed my whole face in the water and blew, then she placed a comforting hand on my chest as I leaned forward and immersed my whole head.

When I leaned on her hand and my head went under, I heard my ears pop, and then I could hear everything happening in the pool: splashing, swishing, clanging. My eyes flew open. It didn't hurt to have water in my eyes, and I could see clearly. I stayed under for close to a minute before I stood up, gasping, to her applause. She looked delighted, and I wanted to jump into her arms.

By Friday, I could float on my back, with Beverly's hand under me to keep my back arched. I could kick around and go from one side of the pool to the other. She taught me the backstroke and pronounced me a swimmer. I wanted to hug her, and she must have seen that, because she reached her arms out at that very moment and hugged me.

Our farewell bonfire Friday night would include an awards ceremony. I had earned four certificates for acing Malcolm's Nature class tests. I knew he would call the names of the winners, and everyone would see us. That fit well with my plans, which were to find some way to stand out so Beverly could remember me.

That afternoon, while some of the counselors were getting their awards ready in the Crafts cabin, Steve held a mini-Olympics for the Athletics classes. I signed up for the running broad jump. My lightweight and strong legs combined to make me a good leaper. But when I got to the field, I almost couldn't go through with my jump. Beverly was going to be marking my landing point. I got my running start, hit my spot perfectly, and sailed seemingly forever. I landed well beyond the second-best jumper, and my jump stood up to the remaining boys'. I had found another way to impress Beverly.

That night, we trooped out to the bonfire pit. Coach Duffy lit the huge stack of firewood, and we sang the camp song. Then came the awards. Forget Archery, Riflery, and Crafts. When Malcolm handed out his certificates, I looked around for Beverly. I didn't see her anywhere. I walked back to my seat with my certificate, proud but not quite as happy as I could had been.

Steve handed out some certificates to the good athletes. I was getting tired and wanted the evening to end, but I had to let everyone else get their awards, since they had to sit while I got mine. Steve looked around and saw me. He spoke again.

"This week, not all of the athletes that impressed me were the fastest ones and the strongest ones. Today, I was really happy to see Seán Dwyer win the running broad jump. He played hard all week, and so I am naming him the Most Enthusiastic Athlete."

My mouth dropped open. I went and took my plaque from Steve, who slapped me on the back. *Where was Beverly?*

Coach Duffy answered that question when he called Beverly up to give her awards. She stood from the far side of the fire, where I had not been able to see her. My heart pounded. She had seen me get my awards.

She distributed certificates to the Advanced swimmers who had completed Red Cross training, and for others who had swum a certain number of laps. I hung on every word she said; I might not ever hear her speak again.

She said, "Now I want to hand out a special award. This week I got to work with a lot of good swimmers, and also I worked with some guys who can't swim at all. One of the guys, and he was one who started the week afraid to put his face in the water, got better really fast, and I was amazed that, at the end of the week, he could float, and he was learning the crawl and the backstroke. I have never been as proud of someone's progress as I am of Seán Dwyer's."

I did not realize she was talking about me until she said my name. I walked to her amid the applause of my fellow campers, and she shook my hand tenderly as she handed me a plaque she had made.

"Great work, Seán."

"Thanks for everything, Beverly."

"Thank *you*, Seán. Good luck. When you go home, practice by putting your head under the water in the bathtub so you don't get scared again."

"I'll do that. It's a great idea. Thanks."

I sat down and looked at my awards. Three plaques and four certificates. I had never experienced anything like it. Beverly had painted my wood plaque with her own hands, on her own time. I would be keeping that one, for sure. As a bonus, I would be able to tell Dad's girlfriend I could swim.

Saturday morning, my Uncle Tom came to camp. He asked if I wanted to stay another week, as Grandma's birthday present to me. I nodded vigorously. I had turned down the same offer when I was ten, but this year, I accepted gratefully. Another week of working with Beverly? Sure.

This week, though, I would be an Advanced Beginner. And that was just the beginning.

Prince of Persia
by Roy Taylor

Head lolling, I lounged in the rusty bed of the faded green pickup beside my older brother, James, who chatted with our two best friends, Dan and Dave. Morning sunlight warmed my closed eyelids, and my thoughts drifted. Spring may be the only tolerable season in Louisiana, a respite wedged between the gray, rain-soaked winter chill that burrows into your marrow and the sweltering, pressure-cooker of summer. For junior high boys, this was a time for dreams, adventure, and the release of pent-up energy. Today, the last Saturday before the end of school, we were headed with our dads to Big Pasture, a loblolly pine plantation owned by Georgia Pacific to feed its pulp mills. The tree farm was big— twenty miles across—and while the trees were small, GP leased fenced sections to cattle farmers for grazing.

Dan and Dave's family lived a mile from our house and attended the tiny country church in Summerville, where Dad ministered. James and I never minded the walk to their place, to be honest, because of their two gorgeous older sisters. Having only recently joined the ranks of adolescents, we boys found the allure of the opposite sex as baffling as it was bewitching. The mini-skirted girls, already in high school, seemingly primped for hours in their bedroom while swaying to the beat of the Beatles and the Beach Boys from their transistor radio. Our furtive gawking and clumsy attempts at conversation must have provided a reliable, if annoying, source of entertainment, which they brushed aside as casually as shooing a fly.

Their father, Jack, tall with thinning brown hair and horn-rimmed glasses, taught high school Social Studies. His true love was their five-acre hobby farm, including a horse, milk cow, pigs, and chickens. For extra income, he ran a herd of Black Angus cattle in Big Pasture.

The previous Saturday, we four boys helped our dads brand and castrate the spring calves. The girls, who tagged along to watch, cheered and jeered when we stripped off T-shirts to expose skinny white chests. What we hadn't anticipated was the challenge of strutting and striking macho poses while dodging fresh cowpies and wrestling bawling, kicking calves to the ground. Desperately clutching the hysterical animals, we hung on as Jack applied a red-hot branding iron to sizzling skin. As acrid smoke— pungent with burnt hair and hide—stung our lungs, we choked and tried not to puke. Even more painful was watching Dad, short and wiry with wavy black hair, wield his knife as deftly as a surgeon to transform bull calves into steers. On impulse, my thighs clenched together while frantic cows lowed their dismay, distraught at the plight of their sons. By the end of the day, Jack hoisted a bucket of Rocky Mountain oysters and offered Dad a half-dozen to take home and fry. Now, our family wasn't squeamish about what we ate. After all, Mom had fixed us everything from armadillo to porcupine. But there are some lines you simply don't cross. To my great relief, Dad turned him down.

Today's foray promised less drama, for which I was grateful. Inspired by a *Farm Journal* article, Jack fancied breeding Brangus beef, a mix of Brahma and Black Angus. Faster-growing, more resilient, and bigger than Black Angus, Brangus were the latest rage for cattle farmers. When a Brahma bull came up for sale at the local auction, he considered the opportunity providential and bought it. Not only did the Brahma come with papers, but a name, Prince of Persia. Jack's only concern was that the bull's horns might be dangerous, and our job today was to correct that.

The truck jounced over a final cattle guard, and I opened my eyes to a burst of spring color. White dogwood, pink magnolia, and blushing crabapple bloomed as brightly as fireworks among dark loblolly pine whose needles splayed out longer than my hand. Pale buds unfurled on iron and scrub oak. Flickering like flames, raucous red cardinals bickered among the green-blossomed branches of sweet gum. Dave adjusted his glasses and pointed to the cloudless sky. "Red-shouldered hawk."

"No, red-tailed," said Dan, shading his eyes with one hand.

"Yup," James agreed. "Tail's red and no checkerboard on its wings."

Dave swiped at his older brother, but Dan, a budding basketball star, easily fended him off.

On the far side of the tallest hill, the pickup swerved off the road, bumped over a shallow ditch, and parked. As we scrambled out, Dave grabbed a cowbell and rattled a signal to the herd that dinner had arrived. Minutes later, a dozen cows with calves streamed out of the woods, one with a clanging cowbell hanging from her neck. Behind the herd marched a colossal beast, gray with a dark face and shoulders as high as my eyes. With every step, his hump swayed behind a thick neck. Elephantine ears swished. Massive muscles rippled. Grunting and snorting, Prince of Persia nosed stragglers into line with finely pointed horns a foot long and two inches across at the base. Curving back and up like fanciful drawings of devils and demons, they evoked terrifying memories of finding myself too close to my grandpa's bull. I backed away.

Jack dropped the tailgate, tossed a hay bale to the ground, and cut the twine. With a snort, the bull tore into the treat while the cows chewed their cuds and shuffled in a circle until Prince was sated.

In response to Jack's nod, Dad casually knotted a rope around the bull's neck. Jack, meanwhile, retrieved the dehorner from his truck. Resembling a medieval torture device, two right-angle blades formed a diamond-shaped guillotine where the tips of stout, four-foot wooden handles came together.

With soft murmurs and pats, Dad coaxed the bull to the truck's rear, where he tied the rope short to the bumper. Not until Jack slid the dehorner over his right horn did the bull sense something was off. Up he reared. Up came the bed of the truck. Back stepped all four boys.

When Jack heaved the handles together, a rack-and-pinion gear drove one of the blades forward across the other. Crunch! The guillotine severed the horn. Earlier that day, I had asked Dad if bulls had feeling in their horns. Any doubt was erased by the earsplitting bellow. Bucking like a rodeo bull, Prince lifted the truck's rear tires clear off the ground. We boys retreated farther away.

Jack spread the handles of the dehorner, and the horn fell to the ground. Fueled by equal parts courage and foolhardiness, he slipped the blades over the rapidly gyrating remaining horn and began to squeeze.

"Bwahh!" the monster bellowed, and with a shake, sent Jack flying. Squatting, the bull snorted and bucked again. Sproing! The bolts on the bumper broke. Prince swung his immense body, waving the dehorner like a club while whirling the rusty bumper, a weapon as deadly as a knight's flail.

Confident that the frothing animal would run off, all six of us stood and waited. I don't know much about how bulls think, but it was soon evident that Prince had unfinished business. No more than ten feet away, he stopped, switched directions, lowered his head, snorted, and charged. Shrieking, we boys sprinted for the truck, vaulted into the bed, and slammed the gate shut. Relieved to reach safety, I sat up, panting, and turned around to a breathtaking panorama of bull anatomy that I would never be able to unsee. Manhood, as long and thick as my forearm, aimed for my heart. Testicles swung halfway to the ground in a sack the size of my fists together. For a long second, the two-thousand-pound beast reared on his hind legs. Clearly, the tailgate provided zero protection. Sharp hooves descended in slow motion, straight toward us boys. There was no way I could move in time. Muscles tightened. Sphincters loosened. I wailed. Someone's hands jerked me to the front of the bed. Wham! Massive hoofs rocked the truck and dented the steel bed on either side of my left thigh. I cried and screamed.

When mighty Prince reared for another strike, Dad's paternal instincts kicked in. Braving the flailing bumper, he grasped the rope and yanked the furious animal to the side. Prince stumbled, snorted, and locked onto his new target. Dropping the rope, Dad sprinted for the front of the truck, the bull kicking up clods of dirt as he gained ground. Dad darted around the grill. Crash! The swinging bumper missed him by inches while demolishing a headlight. Cutting and weaving like an NFL running back, the one-ton mass of bone and muscle closed on his intended victim.

"Whoop, whoop!" Jack shouted, now chasing the bull. Spinning about in a fraction of a second, Prince refocused on Jack. "Aiee!" Jack flew back along the truck, the beast in full pursuit.

Dad seized the opportunity to rip open the driver's door and leap in. Slamming the door shut, he rolled down the window. "Hey, Jack," he hollered, "where's the key?"

"In my pocket!" Jack yelled as he swung around the corner of the truck bed and flung himself out of the bull's path. He fled for the cab, but the animal was too close for him to open the door. Around he ran again, the bull's breath wet and hot on his neck. "Andy," he called, "get ready to open the driver's door."

Whang! The rusty bumper slammed the rear fender as Prince accelerated. Eyes wide, Jack charged past the front grill again and whipped down the side, the bull a step behind. Hurtling into the back on top of us shrieking boys, Jack bellowed, "Open the door now!" and vaulted off the left side of the bed. Dad threw the driver's door open and scooted out of the way in time for Jack to jump in and bang the door shut.

Rrrr, rrr, the starter ground. Wham! The dehorner slammed the cab. *Rrrr. Chug.* The engine coughed to life. Jack desperately rolled up his window. Prince, losing his target, noticed us boys again. He pawed the dirt.

Though we had never stopped screaming, the volume picked up when the raging bull aimed the handles of the dehorner our way. Bloodshot eyes skewered us. Pupils blazed with fury. As though possessed, his entire body radiated a single message. Kill! He pawed the ground. Snort! Lowering his head, the beast streaked our way. We screamed like the devil himself was after us. Maybe, he was.

By chance, the truck was parked facing a small iron oak. The gear shift clunked into reverse. We backed up. The beast pounded closer. Clods of dirt flew. Clunk. The gear shifted into first. The engine roared. Rear tires sprayed dry red clay. Prince was mere feet away.

Crowded against the back of the cab, we cringed when the handle of the dehorner waved above the flimsy tailgate. The truck bounced over the ditch. Clunk. The gears shifted again, and, foot by foot, we pulled away from those murderous eyes. Clunk, Jack shifted into third gear, and as we crested the hill, the bull slowed to a stop.

Slumped like deflated balloons, we gasped for breath and gaped at our nemesis, who loomed tall while glaring down on our craven retreat. As regal as a ruler, at least as regal as his attire allowed, a rusty fender tied to his neck and a four-foot nail clipper attached to his remaining horn, he was Prince of Persia. King of the Hill. Master of his Domain. I was in awe. He had beaten all six of us while hardly breaking a sweat.

I never saw Prince again. A few days later, Dad and Jack coaxed him with a bucket of feed close enough to an iron oak to tie him up, amputate his horn, cut off the rope, and retrieve the bumper. By now, Jack had lost all interest in breeding Brangus. Or even in owning a bull. Not long after, Prince was sold at auction.

Though I didn't read the auction information sheet, I'm guessing it ran something like: Rare opportunity to own a genuine registered Brahma bull. Don't miss this chance to jump onto the profitable Brangus bandwagon. Prince of Persia is guaranteed to inject new vigor into your herd. Though Brahmas are known for their intelligence and gentle nature, for your peace of mind, this magnificent animal has already been dehorned.

One Morning in Chartres
by Beth Kress

At first it was the sound of one voice—
a boy with a knapsack on his back
chanting out a cadence, guiding the troop
coming into view behind him.

Then more voices, growing louder
young French scouts in tan shirts,
navy shorts, and black berets—
boys and girls with bedrolls on their backs
singing marching songs.

On pilgrimage, they've hiked in from many towns,
converging along the old Roman road,
now weaving back and forth
in the courtyard of the massive cathedral
building multilayered human pyramids,
practicing their songs and marching positions—
the commotion sounds of boundless energy.

They straighten their neck scarves and regroup,
hoisting poles with flags of their towns,
and begin to march into the cathedral in formation.
Now their joyous voices begin the French hymn
Appelés Enfants de Dieu
swelling fuller and stronger with each refrain
filling the lofty space, soaring up one hundred twenty feet
to the vaulted ceiling, two thousand voices
creating one resounding hymn of praise.

Joy Street
by Beth Kress

I wonder what it's like
to live on Joy Street
where surely no one is ever mean
or lonely and the neighbors
are all musicians, cyclists, little kids
and people who love to dance.

Far better, it would seem
than living on Heartbreak Hill
or in the town of Boring, Oregon, say
or on Mad Dog Lane in Yorkshire
where you could easily lose your grip.

I'd like to rent flats for all my friends
on Benefit Street
where the living is easy
and they get credit for their kindness.

In a stroke of genius
my friend reserved a plot
in Gate of Heaven cemetery —
the ultimate in strategic moves.

I myself am planning to relocate my family
to a charming road in Loving, Oklahoma
or Why Worry Lane in Arizona —
whichever they prefer.

Let's take our summer vacations
in Friendship, Maine
and spend a month this winter
in Whynot, Mississippi.

I hate to brag, but I myself
do currently live on Mystic Street.

I guess it really is
all about location.

Birdbrain Lessons
by Maurya Simon

You'd think, after living for decades on Mount Baldy, high in southern California's San Gabriel Mountains, that I'd have witnessed or experienced most of the natural wonders and dangers present within our surrounding forests. An avid hiker, I'm blessed to live just minutes from several trails winding up to our prominent peaks, including Mount San Antonio (aka Mount Baldy), a lofty 10,064 feet, the "Three Ts"—Thunder, Telegraph, and Timber Mountains—and Ontario and Cucamonga peaks. I've experienced flash floods and devastating wildfires with subsequent evacuations, and during one solo hike, an avalanche, which I was lucky to survive. Once, while hiking up Bear Canyon, I bumped into a startled eight-point buck—both of us wide-eyed and rendered speechless by our encounter—and on other hikes I've encountered rangy and skittish black bears, sleek gray foxes, bobcat kittens, herds of Nelson bighorn sheep, dancing coyotes, a colorful medley of snakes, droves of blue-bellied western fence lizards and those prehistoric-looking alligator lizards.

I've known bona fide seasons, a treat for any southern Californian: my autumns transformed by the ochres, golds, and amber shades of cottonwoods, maples, and sycamore trees; my winters brightened by dazzling snowstorms and my daughters' laughter as they build buxom snowwomen or sled downhill. During forty years of living in these mountains, I've learned to identify many of our native wildflowers and birds and an array of insects making their homes alongside or inside of mine. I've seen long drought years empty our spring-fed pond, and wet years, like this one, refill it, so friends may toss fish chow to our "pet" rainbow trout, or cruise across the pond's icy waters in an inflatable raft.

Nature holds endless pleasures for Angeles National Forest residents and visitors alike, such as autumn foraging excursions to collect wild blackberries growing alongside San Antonio Creek, or simply dipping one's toes in the crystalline pools in Ice House Canyon, while enjoying a few meditative moments. Early August evenings find locals and down-the-hill folk gathered at Cow Canyon Saddle, far above the Inland Empire's light-polluted skies, heads tilted back and awed by the Perseid meteorite showers. I've friends who drive our winding mountain road in springtime solely to admire the splendid yuccas dotting our mountainsides, their ten-foot flowering spires haloed by happy bees.

There are downsides to living here too: poison oak, bark beetles, trash-can-ransacking "domesticated" bears, periodic power outages, ever-present wildfire threat, floods, rattlesnakes, and gridlocked roads on "snow days" that, in the aftermath of thousands of visitors from the valley below, are littered with tons of refuse. Still, it's not just our splendid wildlife or diverse habitat that keep me tied to these San Gabriel Mountains. It's also our sparkling air and close-knit community, and our environmentally focused public school. Though I've enjoyed other mountain ranges throughout the west, as well as the Himalayas in the distant east, I cherish our unique mountains most, for here winters are so mild that, even on a snowy day, I'll drive a half-hour down to Upland or Claremont to bask in balmy weather under turquoise skies.

Despite having relished a myriad of pleasures gracing my life in the San Gabriel Mountains, it's been the birds—specifically, some Steller's jays—who've taught me how utterly surprising and innovative nature can be. My husband, a transplanted New Yorker, has strung a half-dozen bird feeders outside our picture windows, so whether we're washing dishes in the kitchen, eating lunch in the dining room, or briefly glancing out our living room windows, we're treated to a constant avian parade of hungry juncos, goldfinches, orioles, grosbeaks, flickers, nuthatches, house wrens, and titmice vying for fresh birdseed. Our local Steller's jays, the "heavies" of our front yard aviary, also compete for a place at the bird feeders, but they're craftier than their feathered competitors. Once they've shouldered in among them, the jays will intentionally swing on the feeders to scare off the other birds, simultaneously knocking down and spilling handfuls of seed onto the ground, easier pickings. Or, perched a few yards away, and as they watch wrens and juncos feeding, the jays will also vocally harass these smaller birds attempting to feed, shouting out *shook-shook-shook-shook*, which usually doesn't work to scare them off the feeders. Surely the most vocal species of our mountainous forests, our neighborhood jays proffer a running commentary on the human, canine, and avian activities in our yard throughout the year.

Twenty years ago, I lost a costly and beautiful diamond "tennis" bracelet that my husband had given me for our twentieth anniversary. This well-crafted, gold-chained bauble was so flexible and durable that I was able to safely wear it anywhere, and so I rarely took it off. That late spring day I'd been gardening for a couple of hours, crouched down in my faded jeans, and was lost in thought as I pulled up dandelions, purslane, and lambsquarters. When I went into the house later to shower, I noticed my naked wrist with horror. My husband and I searched the yard for an hour, and then checked it again daily for weeks, but my diamond bracelet was gone.

For a decade, I mourned the loss of this treasured bracelet, believing I'd never see it again. Then, one autumn day after a Santa Ana gale, my husband halted during his cleanup of fallen branches and excitedly called me to come outside. He'd just found a jay's nest in our yard, blown down from a tall pine tree. It was roughly ten inches in diameter and six inches high, a bulky container woven from small sticks, leaves, and moss, and patched together with mud. Its inside was lined with pine needles and tufts of animal hair. And, lo and behold: my dirt-encrusted diamond bracelet was nestled in its inner sanctum, along with some other, glittery things—shreds of gum wrapper foil, a key, and shards from a plastic princess crown. What a windfall! In retrospect, had I been more mindful ten years earlier, I might have looked up and noticed a black-crested cocked head and a pair of greedy eyes carefully watching me while I weeded, the blue-jay's beak curiously silent.

More surprising was the discovery I made five years ago, when a pair of Steller's jays built a nest high up in a Himalayan cedar near our house. That spring, a red-tailed hawk was preying on our neighborhood's birds, so I grew used to hearing its hoarsely shrill cry—*kee-eee-arr*—every dusk. I heard that cry so often, I worried that the hawk had displaced the nesting jays. One day, hearing it once again, I looked up into the pine's lower branches to discover one of the resident jays mimicking the sound of the hawk. The savvy bird was warning me away from its nest by pretending to be a bird of prey. Now here's something even more amazing I've uncovered: since then, each new generation of jays learns to mimic a hawk's cry, thereby warning off potential predators, protecting their young nestlings, and alerting all the other animals in the area to a possible threat. A simple act of ventriloquism has improved the birds' chances for survival, and this behavior keeps getting passed on, year after year.

Initially, we settled in the mountains to escape the lowland valleys' air pollution and extreme summer heat, and because we wanted our daughters to attend Mt. Baldy School, with its nature-centered curriculum. We welcomed the physical challenges of mountain living, and we discovered a welcoming and cohesive community at the same time. As the years pass, my husband and I are learning to savor the more subtle aspects of country life: how the aftermath of a snowstorm creates an almost mystical quiet; how when voles move our tulip-and-daffodil bulbs underground, new flowers erupt every spring in unlikely places; how a loveliness of ladybugs may aggregate in a fallen tree's hollowed trunk; and how the quirky cocking of a Steller's jay's head tells us that it's surveying our labors with both vexation and vested interest. Apparently, after living in these forests for half a lifetime, I'm only just beginning to open my ears and eyes.

In My Garden
by Nancy Canyon

I.
An impenetrable raspberry hedge
abuzz with passels of bombus—
black-and-orange stripes donning
parcels of pollen, readying vines
for sweet berries, seventy-five
plus drupelets each. Later blushed
with summer sun, I will fill pints
with sticky scarlet jam. Heavenly
come winter when the weather
turns cold and gray.

II.
Tiny birds flutter to my garden
gleaning seed from red oakleaf
bolting for the blue. Goldfinches,
once known as lettuce birds, alight
on swaying stalks, hang sideways
and upside down to eat seed
packed along purple stems. I gaze
in rapt silence: flickering wings,
pecking beaks, feeling tickled
the bitter plants have gone to seed.

III.
As tall as me, or perhaps taller,
Russian kale sways, lush with
flowers and hundreds of golden
honeybees. A wonder, this six-foot
forest of brassica. I laugh for real,
Look at that, it's swarming with bees.
Standing close, I watch workers
laden with pollen, buzz in and out
through sprays of yellow flowers.

Kitchen Table
by Nancy Canyon

After school, we sat at the small kitchen table,
dunking graham crackers in cold milk. My brother
and I dunked them long enough to soften, but
not so long to turn soggy and fall in the glass.

In this memory, I don't know why there's a small
table in the middle of the kitchen. We had a breakfast
nook where we ate cereal and slathered boysenberry
jelly on toast, or was it peanut butter?

As a child, I didn't like peanut butter and jelly,
and still don't, so it must have been toast. The best
part of this memory is how hard we laughed when
my brother insisted we were eating poisonberry jelly.

Back to the table in the middle of the kitchen—perhaps
a construction project, a renovation of the breakfast
nook, or maybe the table migrated in my memory.
I have another memory of my brother and me rolling

oranges on that table, working until pulp became juice.
We then poked a hole through the rind and sucked down
the sweet nectar, massaging the fruit, swallowing every
drop. We laughed then too. I can still hear us now.

Old Growth
by Nancy Canyon

~on a line from Robert Frost

The woods are lovely, dark and deep,
ravens croak, wings flap,
clumps of lungwort lichen
swirl downward, landing in
dense thickets of huckleberry.
A ripening dream calls me to follow the
spongy path spiced with old growth needles,
winding through giant trees that have lived
for hundreds of years. I place my palms
against a massive trunk and listen to the tree's heart,
listen deeply to my old friend, the cedar,
listen deeply to the giant's wisdom.
Listen deeply to the ancient one.

Searching for My Spiritual Roots
by Linda Morrow

On an October Sunday in 1945, sunshine streamed through three large windows and left patterns on the tiled floor of the children's classroom of the First Parish Unitarian Church in Needham, Massachusetts, a Boston suburb. Holding my hand, my mother bent down and said reassuringly, "See Jane sitting over there? It looks like she's saving the seat next to her for you. You'll be just fine and I will be here to pick you up when class is over."

I nodded, let go of Mommy's hand and walked over to where children, seated in a circle on small wooden chairs, chatted quietly. I wasn't nervous. I went to kindergarten five mornings a week and loved it, so Sunday School should be easy. Right? No fuss, no bother.

I settled onto the seat next to my best friend Jane, and listened attentively as our teacher, Mrs. Patterson, went over the plans for the next hour. "We'll open with our song, go around the circle for greetings and introductions, and have our Bible story. Then after the offering, we will go outside to look for items to add to our "Signs of Fall collection."

I smiled inwardly to myself . . . *singing, morning hello, story time and then outside . . . Just like kindergarten.* I wasn't sure what an offering was, but figured I'd find out soon enough. We all stood up to sing a song about Jesus loving us. I didn't know the words, but caught on to the chorus pretty quickly. During introductions, when it was my turn, I said my name nice and loud. "Linda Jean Morrow."

Story time was fun. Mrs. Patterson told us about a man named Noah. I really liked the way she used pictures, which stuck like magic to the board next to her. Noah looked a bit strange to me. His dark hair was mostly covered by a cream-colored cape which fit tightly around his head and flowed down his back. His bushy beard rested on a red-and-white-striped robe, sorta like Daddy's bathrobe, but longer. It almost covered the funny-looking shoes made of straps on his feet. God told Noah to build an ark and fill it with pairs of animals. I'd never heard of an ark, but Mrs. Patterson stuck a picture on the board which looked like a boat with a roof on it. She asked if we wanted to guess what kinds of creatures Noah gathered. "Tigers!" "Lions!" "Elephants!" "Birds!" Soon the board was filled with all kinds of animals. Mrs. Paterson continued the story. After the animals and Noah's family were on the boat, God made it rain for forty days and forty nights! But all were safe from the flood 'cause they were on the boat. I felt glad that everyone survived. Next, Mrs. Patterson taught us a song about how pretty the earth was. "For the beauty of the earth, for the beauty of the skies . . ."

Then it was time for the offering. Mrs. Patterson took out a shiny silver plate, put some money in it, and passed it to the kid sitting next to her. Around the circle went the plate. By the time it got to me, it was filled with coins.

"Oh . . ." I thought. "What a nice way to welcome me to Sunday School." I reached in with one hand and grabbed a fistful of money. Jane's chestnut eyes opened wide, and she tugged on one of her braids, but she said nothing. And then it was time to go outside!

My first experience with a church offering became a family legend, a story Jane and I have recalled with much hilarity many times during more than eighty years of friendship.

Over the next several years, my parents were active and involved members at First Parish Unitarian. Dad sang in the choir. At home I'd often sing along with him as he practiced hymns for the upcoming Sunday service. My mother served as superintendent of the children's religious education program and made certain I had money for the weekly offering. Each summer, she attended a retreat sponsored by the Unitarian Northeast District on Star Island off the New Hampshire coast. She returned energized and eager to add new programs to the curriculum.

During the first several years of Sunday School, those ubiquitous Old Testament flannel board Bible stories formed the nexus of our lessons. The characters and their actions fascinated me: Adam and Eve, Noah and the Ark, Joseph and his Coat of Many Colors, Sampson and Delilah, David and Goliath, Daniel and the Lion's Den. I remember being especially intrigued by all the stories about Moses: how as a baby he'd survived by being hidden in the bulrushes; how he led his people out of Egypt by parting the Red Sea; the burning bush; his receiving the Ten Commandments.

When Jane and I were in fourth grade, my mother added field trips to the program. Our class visited other places of worship: a Catholic Cathedral with its soaring arches and stained glass windows; a synagogue where the men covered their heads with hats and the women sat in a separate section; an AME (African Methodist Episcopal) church and its lively call-and-response congregants and rollicking gospel music; the spare interior of a Quaker Meeting House and the profound silence. Those encounters left me with the realization that people interacted with God in many different ways.

I also became aware that I experienced Jesus in a different way than most of my public school friends. I can remember saying to one, "I'm a Unitarian. We don't believe in Jesus." Of course, that wasn't true, but it was my way of explaining my Nontrinitarian religious education.

But regular church attendance ended for me at age ten when our family moved to the seashore town Marshfield, Massachusetts, in 1950. There, we joined the North Community Church, but it was never with the same vigor or commitment. By the time I was in high school, my main interest was the Sunday night open gym where the youth group met to play pickup basketball. My basketball skills improved, but over the next sixty years I didn't own a Bible and rarely set foot inside a church. My spiritual roots were planted at First Parish Unitarian, but then left untended for a very long time.

Decades later, two shattering events changed my life forever.

The first occurred in 2015 when my eldest son Steve, who was born with Down Syndrome, died at age forty-nine. I'd been told shortly after his birth that he was unlikely to outlive his teens. While he certainly proved medical experts wrong, his passing was sudden and without warning. He woke up one morning and left his condo with his community access aide to run some errands. When he began coughing up blood, he was rushed to the hospital emergency room, but his heart stopped as personnel began treatment to discover the source of bleeding. As news of Steve's passing spread, some Christian friends responded. "He's with God now." "Steve's been made whole."

These well-meaning condolences left me devastated. I envied their certitude, but unable to share it, longed for a spiritual home. I was missing something, but didn't know where to turn.

The 2016 Presidential election intensified my desire for internal, sacred understanding. I found the new political/religious climate not only confusing but offensive. How could people who called themselves Christians be so uncaring, so full of hatred toward those who lived on the margins of our society—as Steve had? At a social gathering I asked a friend with a strong religious foundation, "What would Jesus do if he met Trump?"

"Probably ask him to dinner," Nancy replied. My raised eyebrows indicated I had no idea what her answer meant. Then she followed with a question of her own. "Would you like to do a Bible study with me?"

I hesitated, and then surprised myself by answering, "Yes. Yes, I would." I knew many Old Testament stories thanks to Mrs. Paterson's felt board, but I'd never really read the Bible.

And so we began meeting regularly: myself, a lesbian agnostic, and Nancy, an Evangelical Christian, who did not identify with the rabid religious right. We were united by our strong sense of social justice and a deep mutual respect for each other. Nancy loaned me a Bible and we began by reading the gospel of John. Progress was slow. I had so many questions. Nancy was patient.

Each meeting ended with Nancy praying—something which initially made me uncomfortable and self-conscious. But with time, my disquiet eased as I realized that Nancy's prayers were really quite straightforward. She spoke what was in her heart: her gratitude, her concerns, her desires, acknowledgement of her shortcomings. One day, when Nancy ended her prayer, I added my own. I asked for support for people I cared about, help with questions I had, guidance for an upcoming decision. Prayer was possible for me! I felt a burden lift.

We were still working our way through the Gospel of John when the pandemic hit and our meetings stopped. Without Nancy's guidance, her Bible sat on my bookshelf gathering dust.

In June of 2021, the second transformative event occurred. After experiencing bouts of gastric discomfort, exploratory testing resulted in a diagnosis of advanced stage esophageal cancer. Without treatment, life expectancy was six-to-eight months. With treatment, the five-year survival rate was twenty percent. At eighty-one, I knew I valued quality of life over quantity. What did this turn of events mean? What was I supposed to learn from this?

My efforts to understand and embrace my spirituality intensified. Cancer can do that for you. In addition to resuming in-person meetings with Nancy, I also met with a woman who at age seventy-seven had become an ordained Zen Buddhist priest. From her, I learned the importance of staying in the present and started a very rudimentary meditation practice. My main take-away? I was not in control. So who was?

I decided to seek treatment, which meant several weeks of radiation and chemotherapy followed by major surgery. For the remainder of 2021, I listened to various recorded meditations, but I was too sick to continue meeting with Nancy.

By the spring of 2022, I finally felt well enough to resume my sessions with my mentor. We finished reading John. For me, the key point was Jesus's many acts of loving generosity and his acceptance of all—regardless of their station in life. I felt a strong sense of peace within me.

Next, at my request, we focused on the Old Testament. Time and time again, I recognized various phrases, parables, characters, stories. I surprised Nancy as well as myself by dredging up the lyrics to different hymns I sang with my dad in the distant past. Clearly the five-and-a-half years I spent attending Sunday School at First Parish Unitarian had had an impact on me. Those long-neglected roots began poking through my conscience, demanding acknowledgement.

So where has this period of reflection about my long-ago church experiences, coupled with my meetings and discussions with Nancy, left me? I cannot know what the future holds for me. I am at peace with that. But my spiritual quest has transformed me in some foundational ways. While my sexuality hasn't changed, I'm no longer willing to label myself an agnostic. I believe in a Higher Power. Do I call this God? Goddess? Or as Anne Lamott puts it, GUS (Great Universal Spirit)? It doesn't matter. I know this Force exists.

I'm more comfortable with the concept of prayer. I have a routine I follow each night after getting into bed which includes saying the twenty-third psalm several times while dedicating it to various individuals or groups. I change the gender of the pronouns depending on the people for whom I am praying. I follow the psalm with a personal mantra:

May I be safe and protected from danger.
May I be happy. May I be kind.
May I be healthy in mind and body, resilient and strong.
May I live with ease, in peace and contentment.
And when my time comes . . .
May I want what I have, do what I can, and be who I am.

This time of reflection each night brings me to a place of tran-quility and profound gratitude.

These days, I work at remembering to stay in the present and live my life. I experience the joy of being less judgmental—of myself and others. I've learned how to extend grace and compassion to myself. I worry less about what others think of me. All I can do is my best. I've found a fortitude I didn't know I had thanks to the support of friends and family. And perhaps most importantly, I continue to see diversity as a strength as I believe Jesus did. I believe our Higher Power does, as well. There are so many ways to live a good and gracious life. All people have worth, and it is my job to see that worth in everyone.

Nancy's Bible sits on the coffee table and I refer to it frequently along with other readings either she or I come across. Our weekly discussions both increase my knowledge and raise many questions as I expand my comprehension about a period of history and a culture previously unknown to me. As I continue to deepen my spirituality, I am curious to see where my search for spiritual truth takes me. I continue to struggle with acceptance of a Trinitarian belief construct. Perhaps a testament to my Unitarian heritage? I don't see regular church attendance in my future, however, any time I spend outdoors contemplating nature's beauty nourishes me.

Development of my religious beliefs is a work in progress, but I trust wherever I end up will be the right place for me. I am grateful for the awakening of my spiritual roots and the role they play in my daily life. Healing from trauma isn't linear, but Steve's death and my cancer have enriched my life in unexpected ways, and for that I am eternally thankful.

Bliss
by Carol McMillan

Bliss is chocolate-covered,
golden-flavored
nestled deep where
life glows warm.
Touching pathways unexplored
when we incarnate.
Pathways followed
only with my soul.

Lighter than
Earthly substance,
my essence floats,
flows, seeps, flies.
A movement so exquisite
I barely touch its essence
in this form we call "living."

I have done this before.
Traveled this path.
Funny that we don't remember.
That we fear death,

yet I am alive, and somehow
I do know it.
I have tasted bliss in
the flavor of a sunrise.

Smelled the aroma of a song.
Felt the color of a moonbeam,
Heard bud growth, new in spring,
and seen bliss
in the utter darkness
that glows
and flows in spirals
when I look within.

Beauty in a word.
Blessing in a concept.
Beyond intellect.

Beside thought.
Before mind.
Between life and birth.
Between death and breathing,
bliss appears.
It carries us
in filmy blankets,
thinner than fairy wings,
softer than angel breath,
carries us
with the sweetest compassion,
tasting of dark cherry juice
picked from a tree.

I wait.
Bliss cannot be conjured.
A gift of grace
unearned.
Bliss simply reaches out
and takes me when
I least expect.

I watch
and wait.

Apple Blossom Time
by Debu Majumdar

I remembered Father's words: "*Bleiben immer in Bewegung.*" He said that on my twelfth birthday in 1944 when we passed Markdorf near Lake Constance—"Always keep moving." We lost our parents two months later, but since then, I had pushed Peter, my eight-year-old brother, on and on through all the devastation in the southern part of Germany. We kept on running, not knowing why, not knowing where to go, running away from something that neither of us understood.

"Peter, Peter, *steh auf!*" I nudged him. "Get up!"

He stirred a little but made no attempt to rise.

"It is a good day outside, not cold."

"Let me stay in bed a little more."

"We'll be late and miss out. You don't want that."

He opened his eyes and I pulled him up by his hands.

Peter put on a shirt he found in a house we'd searched the day before and followed me out.

The sun was up. I glanced back at the bombed-out house where we'd slept, the top all but gone. Most buildings in this little town were heavily damaged. Our room had solid walls and a ceiling unlike the unstable buildings around us. The area had been bombed some time back. There was no sign of anyone. We marched on. We had found a place the day before yesterday—just by chance—where we could get something hot to eat.

"Peter!" I urged him. "We must go there quickly before it is too late!"

We walked on the wide path that was once a decent road. Chunks of blacktop remained here and there. Shells and heavy-armored vehicles had created big holes and cracks. I saw large craters in the distance. Passing by buildings scorched with black burn marks, no windows intact anywhere, we moved on, increasing our speed.

"That's a better one." Peter pointed out a house. "We should explore it. Maybe we can find something to eat."

We entered the building, still solid and erect. "They were rich," Peter said. "They must have escaped before the bombs came."

I didn't say anything. Strange, no one had looted the place. We ran to the kitchen and pulled the refrigerator handle; inside, it was empty. Others had come before us. No clothes remained in the house, but people hadn't ruined it. The tables, chairs, beds, and such things were left intact.

At the beginning, many people trudged the road, now very few. We had no idea what had happened to them or where they had gone. I had followed Father's last words: "Keep moving." Recently, the noise had stopped, silence all around—no bombs, no shells, no screams, no running people. We hadn't noticed at first, but it had been quiet for several days. Then we stayed put, because we had found a nearby location for hot food—such a rare thing. We hadn't had anything warm to eat for weeks. My steps became faster. We must not be late. Even a minute could be too late. "Peter, come on. We mustn't let them outrun us."

After a while, Peter said, "Look there. I see the red roof."

His words lifted me. I saw the farm in the distance, the outline of a sizeable house, and I felt hopeful. "Yes, Peter. We are near."

Soon, my view of the back of the large farmhouse became clearer. This was where we first saw them running. We didn't realize what they were running for. Then we understood . . . but all the food was quickly gone. It was good that we didn't come to the front of the house; we wouldn't have discovered the food. We would not have knocked at the front door anyway, the Alsatian dogs or guards with guns would have chased us away. We hung around at the back, but no more food came out during the day.

"You know what to do, right?" I asked Peter.

"Yes. First, let's get as close as we can."

There was no sign of any animals in the field. "Good," I told Peter, looking around. "I hope they're far away."

We got closer and recognized our target, a small gray door near the ground, two farm barrels nearby and some large farm equipment. "You know," I told Peter, suddenly fearful, "that pigs can smell food from far away."

My heart started to beat faster as I saw the thick leather flap over the small opening to keep the pigs from getting into the house. We stood quietly about twenty yards away. After some waiting, I heard noises from inside. "Get ready, Peter," I whispered.

We saw the flap open, and we ran toward it. A load of fire-burnt potatoes came out. Warm vapor emanated from them. Peter picked up one and hissed, "Uh! Too hot." He dropped it.

The potatoes were roasted on an open fire and dumped through the opening. Another load came out. I picked up one. Too hot. I heard a noise and glanced back. "The pigs are coming," I shouted. "Peter, pick up two and run. They'll be here in a minute." I started to run toward the fence.

Peter cried and I looked back. He had almost collided with a pig he didn't see come at him from the side. He avoided it but then stumbled. His potato fell out of his hand. He got up quickly, picked up the potato and ran. I was so happy he didn't lose it.

The pinkish-white pigs surrounded the leather flap, shoving each other. Some small and some enormous, all fighting for a share of the coveted potatoes. Some grunted, some squeaked, some barked. They gobbled the potatoes with their little tails wagging.

Safely away from the farm pigs, we sat at the edge of the almost obliterated road and ate our warm potatoes—two large ones for each of us—perhaps with more pleasure than the pigs. They were half-baked, a little burnt, but the heat was still cooking inside of the potatoes, making them softer—the most wondrous food in the world.

"Isn't it great," Peter said, "that we found this place?"

I nodded and enjoyed the moment of gorging on the potatoes, filling my starved stomach. I relaxed and gazed at the large field. No thought for the rest of the day entered my mind. I was at peace. I spotted some green shoots in the soil. The farmer had tilled and seeded the field. I saw the long rows and furrows, and imagined plants would soon sprout. The field would be green in a few weeks. New growth: what a change from all the destruction we had seen. A hopeful feeling spread over me. We had not seen green fields for a long while. I tried to remember when I had last played with friends in such a field.

I kept on gazing at the field. Then a thought came to me. We hadn't heard any planes overhead or the distant sound of shelling for some time. Had the war ended?

A gentle fragrance floated in the air, energizing my hope. Perhaps the war was over, and we didn't know. I looked toward the other side of the road where the fragrance came from and saw white buds covering short trees. Beautiful little white flowers in bunches—pale with reddish-pink undersides. I stared at the trees in amazement. "Peter," I said softly, "apple trees have blossomed."

A subtle breeze, reminiscent of honeysuckle, pulled me toward the orchard. Or was it a fragrance of all the flowers in the world—rose, jasmine, lily of the valley, and hyacinth? I forgot about land mines and started to walk toward the orchard. An indescribable joy filled my heart. The blossoms were a hopeful sign of a promising future.

"Peter, Peter, see all around!" I danced up and down, my heart swelling with happiness. The words my beloved teacher had admired so much came to me, "*Alle Menschen werden Brüder.*" My heart beat with longing and the poem reverberated in my mind.

Let us sing more cheerful songs,
More songs full of joy!
Joy!
Joy!
Thy magic power re-unites
All that custom has divided,
All men become brothers,
Under the sway of thy gentle wings.

—Beethoven Symphony 9 choral, translation by Aaron Green

Fruitful
by Wendell Hawken

In the long sweet not-too-far-back
language from, say, Dr. Williams' chilled plums,
double dare of eaten peach,
midcentury maraschino cherries bobbing
lonesome in a Midwest fridge,
now the twenty-first century tree-ripe plums
beside a Philadelphia street.
                    No. Not plums.
I checked myself (which more and more
these days I do). It's figs,
figs dirtying the sidewalk intersection
of a named and numbered street.
You could go there some September as a pilgrim,
a poetic pilgrim
seeking the sweet soft red-streaked flesh
because I believe in the poem.
If not in life, then license.
                    If you google *fig tree poem*
and can get past Sylvia *sitting*
in the crotch of this fig tree (though prose)
if you resist clicking down Sylvia's path—
too sad for early morning—
                    if you stick with figs,
not the *Ficus religiosa* under which Buddha
found enlightenment, it is *Ficus carica*
you want sticky fingers to stick to,

not necessarily believing its sap removes warts,
softens calluses. Or its seeds
the seeds of understanding, unity, and truth.
Female fertility.
And as a fig leaf is said to cover shame
and in fact now covers Uffizi statuary penises
(thanks to Popes who had the original
phalluses chiseled off)
Much to answer for, those popes.
             And there's always the knowing
bite in Adam's throat, bob and swallow,
going nowhere.
Whereas my mind more and more
the goat going where it will and turns
from morning news—floods, bridge collapse,
impending war—
                   to fig tree joy as jump-start
for my own—like begetting like
                        savoring every fig tree word,
inserting myself beneath that tree
slurping figs with strangers
while in this warm house, both dogs at my feet,
waiting for their walk into blue snow morning.
             Yesterday, a red fox crossed the yard
slipping here and there on ice to disappear in
the scrub woods that flanks the house.
                        How exposed it seemed,
how protective I felt
discovering Sylvia's school-girl diary
and her college letters
there on display in the Grolier Club's glass windows
for anyone who wandered down 60th Street
any time of day or night to read.
Though I read them.
Read every word.

Alive
by Wendell Hawken

I am alive.
I have my hair
and clever lungs pink and puffy in and out.

I am lighter than before, light where light has never been
where you were, dead thing.

It is early,
Unrisen morning.
Songbirds lick their voices at the dead thing in my hand.

Lord how I love this birdsong, how it licks into the quiet places,
licks the morning yellow under custard-colored sky.

I am sorry you have died, dead thing, and cannot come
after berries I would pick
to feed you one by one, strawberries,

to fill the bucket up for home
for tea with mother's milk, sugar sucked from island cane
chattering the fishbone cup.

Imagine, dead thing of the rhythmic dark, how strawberries
wear their seeds upon their skin
symmetrical and sweet for anyone to see.

This summer's good, especially good, for berries,
strawberries.

I stuff my mouth with berries.

Embracing an End
by Dawn Quyle Landau

Over the nearly ten years I've worked at Whatcom Hospice House, I have come to view death in unexpectedly positive ways. While no life is a straight line, I've discovered that death rarely follows a straight line, either. In accepting the many ways hospice care can change the trajectory of both, I've learned that death can be positive, on so many levels, for both those who are dying and those of us still living.

On a regular basis people say to me, "I can't imagine doing that (work); it must be so hard." It's almost predictable, the moment I share that I've volunteered at hospice for so many years. No one ever says, "How uplifting!" And yet, for me, it is. It is positive and nourishing on deeply spiritual levels. It's work that leaves me energized and fulfilled after every shift—even after the shifts that gut me and take every ounce of energy. I may walk in feeling tired, or cranky, but I always walk out profoundly grateful and appreciative of the connections I've made; the graceful and meaningful dance I share with the hospice team; contented in having made a difference; and reenergized in having shared such sacred space with people at the end of their lives.

The stories that leave me breathless are simple on the surface, but I've come to appreciate them for the unicorns they are—the patients who say: "I had such a happy childhood; my parents were so loving and taught us to really live life with gusto"; "I grew up feeling so lucky!"; "My husband/wife and I had such a wonderful marriage"; "I really have been so fortunate to be healthy and live independently for so long"; "I'm ready to die; I know I'll be reunited with loved ones; this is just the next step in a very happy life." Rainbows, and sparkling unicorns.

Death and I have a long and enmeshed relationship. We were introduced when I was very young, and death shook my entire world. When I was ten, my father was killed in a car accident, and I was left wondering how love could be so shockingly withdrawn in an instant. Poof! Just like that, all of the magic and wonder I felt, the sense that I was precious and important, seemed to vanish with him. As a child, I could not comprehend that this love would live beyond that terrible day, sustaining me for decades beyond his life. At the time, it was simply a cruel and unfathomable shift in my universe. That loss was followed by four more painful deaths in two years, and a difficult home life with our mother, a dramatic shift from the loving one my father provided. All of this left me, at twelve, saying my nightly prayers and telling God, in no uncertain terms, that I now knew he was not real—or that he was a cruel and unseeable force I no longer wanted in my life. As I sat at my window, I distinctly remember hoping that this prayer hurt God as much as I believed he had hurt me. My deep wounds were camouflaged by a clear, vindictive rage, directed at the North Star, Polaris, where I was sure he dwelled.

Over the years, I stopped attributing everything to the workings of an omnipotent man in the sky. I called myself an atheist for a while—something that made adults laugh, coming from my preteen self—then an agnostic, and then I just stopped talking about religion. But death was something that followed me. It wasn't as shocking; it became less personal, but I knew not to let my guard down, regardless of all the beauty I found in life. Despite the mystery of a forest, the beauty of the marsh where I lived, or the endlessness of the ocean, death was always the period at the end of the sentence.

In 2011, with children who were getting older and my role as central operations director at home narrowing down, I applied to do the then lengthy training to be a hospice volunteer. Admittedly, I had little-to-no experience with hospice. I didn't know what a volunteer would do, or why this would be a good fit for me. I wanted to do something structured that would help in the community; death whispered in my ear; hospice seemed interesting. The training schedule was surprisingly long and had a lengthy wait-list; I was disappointed to learn that it would be about a year before I could start—early 2012. Instead, last minute, we took in two foreign exchange students for the 2011/12 school year, and I put hospice on the back burner. I shuttled three teens; I started a blog; I balanced friends and home with caring for my mother, who was in the late stages of Huntington's Disease. I figured I'd sign up for training the next year.

Then my mother fell and broke her elbow. That wouldn't be a death sentence for most people, but in her case it was. It required a fairly simple surgery, rehab and recovery, but during her hospital stay, Mom confided to the doctors that she wanted to die. This was not shocking news. I understood her feelings. In fact, had "death with dignity," or assisted suicide, been legal in Washington at the time, I would have supported that option. It sounds cavalier, but our family had already been horribly impacted by Huntington's Disease; we knew her death would be slow and cruel. We knew there were no silver linings or bright sides to look for. She knew these things too. I would not have stopped her from making such a decision. However, that option was legal in Oregon, not Washington, and I was not willing to sneak down to Oregon to help Mom end her life.

The new palliative care doctor where we lived made it *easier* when she shared my mother's feelings with my husband and me and said these clear and straightforward words: "Your mother does not want to live any longer with her illness; her quality of life is diminishing rapidly, and she does not want to struggle through rehab and pretend otherwise. If she gets in bed, and we make her comfortable, she will not live long."

Easier. And much harder. I had a million questions, many of which could not be answered until we moved forward. *How long would it take for her to die?* That was impossible to say, but not more than a few months. *What would that look like?* With her Huntington's, doctors had previously told us to expect two-to-three more years, with many falls, decreased cognitive skills, and punishingly long days for my mother—filled with frequent stitches and broken bones from the falls; the inability to speak clearly or enjoy much anymore, and loneliness that we could not fully ease. She was sixty-seven years old. *Would she suffer? Was this ethical?* She still occasionally enjoyed drives to see the fall colors or watch the water, and dinners with us, I reasoned, but I also knew my mother rarely wanted to go out anymore. She loved us all, but often couldn't—or didn't want to—follow or participate in conversations. She felt both bitter about having Huntington's and not getting to live the life she imagined, and equally apathetic. *Where would she go? Would she die in our home? And what? And what?* There were a million questions; hospice gave me the answers.

Within a week, she was approved for our local Hospice House and moved into room six at the house I now know so intimately and completely that it's hard to believe I was so lost at the time. Most of what I bring to my job now, I learned as a family member over the three full months my mother spent at Hospice House, from October until 4:21 a.m., New Year's Eve, 2011. As a family member, I believed it was my responsibility to get a washcloth, something to drink, another blanket, or whatever Mom needed moment by moment, as I loosely balanced my days getting the kids off to school (our teen son, and the two exchange students, who'd arrived three weeks before Mom fell), spending all day at Hospice House, racing home to make dinner, and going back each night, until she fell asleep—every day, for three months. I refused help, other than medical assistance, every time the staff offered. I barely noticed the volunteers, in a blur of coming and going and trying to keep all the balls in the air.

I spent days lying in bed with Mom, watching the shows I'd grown up on: *Little House On the Prairie*, *The Waltons*, *The Brady Bunch*, and *Mary Tyler Moore*—shows that sucked us both back into years that had been challenging and toxic, but were softened by these idealistic shows. She relaxed in my arms as I silently processed my feelings. We were anchored in the present, in that safe and quiet room . . . as we waited for Mom to die.

She held on, and on, and on, as we watched TV, sat in silence, talked, watched more TV, discussed whether she wanted a funeral, to be buried or cremated (cremated and put in the water), what she regretted, what I still wanted from her—clarity, truth, explanations for the ways her choices and actions had impacted me. She held on as her body dropped below ninety pounds, as she discussed the things she was willing to examine, and listened as we said what we needed to say. She sipped Coke on ice but had notes all over her room, asking visitors and staff not to ask her if she was hungry. In the end, she essentially died of starvation of her choosing. I've learned that a human can go without food, but rarely survives more than three-to-five days without fluids. Each tiny sip of Coke prolonged my mother's life. She was quiet most of the time, but still ornery and independent enough to tell the Threshold Choir, a volunteer group that croons at dying people's besides, that she hated their "soothing" music. "I don't want them in here," she croaked, "I feel like they're singing me to death." My mother never minced her words. But she wouldn't let go.

I didn't eat any of the fresh-baked cookies that volunteers baked several times a day. I didn't eat any of the Thanksgiving food from the family room, even as my stomach growled; I presumed it was for staff, not families. I didn't ask for anyone to sit with my mother. "I've got it" I said, over and over again. I put ointment on her cracked lips. I rubbed lotion on her dry skin. I brushed her thick hair and held her whenever she seemed to need it. I did not let Hospice do what I now know they do so well. I did not let them do more of the work so that I could simply be her daughter—maybe I felt better reverting to the caretaker I'd long been for her, as the eldest child of a woman who was widowed with three children when she was twenty-nine. I jumped in and tried to fix what couldn't be fixed, and learned so many things as I lived on autopilot.

But Hospice got it. They kept offering. They treated my mom with dignity and gentle care. They accepted her ornery. They smiled and said "okay" when I said we were fine, over and over. They reassured me that they were right outside if we needed them. I took it all in, and after my mother finally died—in thirty of the most transformative minutes of my life—I knew I wanted to do that work too. I had noticed every detail in those three months, and wanted to help others in this process. I waited two weeks after Mom's death, went back to sign up for the course, and was promptly informed that I would have to wait a year, as they did not accept anyone who was actively grieving.

I was annoyed. I felt I'd long processed the complex feelings I had. Her death was not a surprise. But the rules were firm, and as the months passed, I realized I was not as free and clear of grief as I'd thought.

Death is interesting that way. Its sidekick, grief, is equally tricky. Grief waxes and wanes. Months after her death, I still found myself reaching for the phone to tell Mom something or feeling a vague sense of panic when I realized we hadn't invited her over for dinner in ages. I was fine, I reasoned, but that year of processing ultimately made me a better hospice worker when I finally took the course in the fall of 2013, a year and a half after Mom died. All the things I hadn't wanted for myself, I realized I could offer to others.

I started my time at Whatcom Hospice House believing that my long history with death would make me a better volunteer. To a point, that's been true. However, it's what I learned when Hospice was caring for my mother, and what I've learned from each of the thousands of patients and families I've now worked with, that has allowed me to see this work as deeply rewarding. While loss will probably always have pain attached to it, death can be gentle and affirming. People in the final months, weeks, or hours of their lives can discover new things about themselves. They can let old wounds go and find peace around hard things they thought they'd take with them. Families can find closure and love in broken spaces.

This is not always true. I have seen plenty of angry people who go into *that dark night* holding on to all of the wrongs and slights they've carried through their lives. I've seen children who aren't speaking to parents, spouses who say horrible things to each other as the clock ticks down, and pain piles on pain. "Jesus, Betty! You're dying. Stop acting like you're going home." When an abusive husband said this to his dying wife, it was not my place to tell him how awful I thought he was. I held Betty's hand, and reassured her that she'd done the best she could for herself and her husband, and that I would sit with her as she struggled with her demons. Betty held my hand tightly for hours, and died that evening with another volunteer by her side. Ultimately, I've seen more of the former than the latter, but I can help a death be gentler.

Each week, when I arrive at Hospice House, death is my bitch. My past has empowered me in this work. I will not be blindsided; I know that the people I care for will die—maybe not today, but soon—regardless of whether I get attached to them or barely know them. However, I also know that I can give death a run for its money. I let families know that their loved ones are not made of paper. They can touch them and speak meaningful words in their ears. Recently, a patient's wife broke down. Clutching my hands and crying, she told me that she just wanted to wrap herself around her husband.

"He is the finest man I've ever known. He has made me feel special for nearly thirty years," she told me.

"Ann, you can hold him any way that makes you both happy. You can get into bed with him and wrap him up, just the way you want to," I told her as we held hands and she cried.

An hour later, when I came in to see if her husband John wanted anything, the two of them were entwined in the most loving knot in his bed. John smiled at me with tears in his eyes, "Thank you so much for talking to my beautiful bride."

I share the science of death with patients and their families. Hearing is the last thing to go, and many studies show that the brain keeps processing for three-to-thirteen minutes after the heart stops. Think about that. It's astonishing, to know that when our hearts stop, our brains may still be processing the last words we heard. I tell them that I believe even the most "unresponsive" patient is still there with us. "This is why I always touch them when I come in, and tell them I'm here." I believe it matters so much what those last words are, and that we treat each person with dignity.

It's inspirational beyond explanation to know that death doesn't have to be traumatic. It still is sometimes. People will continue to die traumatically like my father did. Young people will die too soon. Good marriages will be cut short. Bad marriages will be left unresolved. Spouses, parents, grandparents, siblings, aunts, uncles, and friends will struggle with the fact that death is a period we can't avoid at the end of countless sentences. But now I know so much more about how that can be reexamined and addressed. I don't fear death. I don't want to face it any time soon, but I know I can look it in the eye and accept it. I feel hopeful that I will one day feel at peace with that moment in my life, that I'll say, "I'm okay with this; I'm ready," and pass on to the next unknown phase peacefully. I've come to see life and death as a continuum. Each week when I finish my shift, I feel joy and pride in not minimizing this uniquely individual experience, in knowing I often help others feel less fearful or shaken by an event that society still broadly avoids and characterizes as negative. I feel uplifted in viewing life more fully, more beautifully, through coming to terms with and embracing death.

Good Will, Glad Tidings
by Brenda Wilbee

Years ago, my sister gave me two sets of four decorative napkin rings made of brass with large costume jewels for pizazz. In one set, the center oval "gem" was ruby, the other set, emerald. Surrounding these eye-catchers—cut into a dozen or more facets to catch light and sparkle—other plastic jewels danced like ring-around-the-rosie. Pearls. Cubic zirconia. Amber. Designed, of course, to deck out a Christmas dinner table with all the fa-la-la-la-la of Yuletide. Very festive, very bright. Except for me they were a bit too gaudy to go with my Great-Aunt Vi's century-old dining room suite, and so for years, the napkin rings sat in the top drawer of her antique buffet. Each year, I'd open the drawer to get some candles, see them in their corner, and debate with myself. Each year it was the same answer: No, not this Christmas.

The napkin rings followed me pillar to post as life evolved, each time packed and unpacked and packed again. Auntie's dining room suite too. Aunt Vi was the aunt every child should have. Walks to the beach, forts made from washed-up logs, long-tailed kelp turned into dolls, pebbles for eyes. For my real doll, she knitted dresses, bonnets, and booties. Aunt Vi loved and laughed and made things sing. Only she had ever seen my imaginary friend. I faithfully dusted and polished her lovely dining set made from black walnut, a table, a buffet, and a china hutch, keeping my aunt alive in my mind with each wipe of the cloth. The years passed, and every time I moved, a vague concern popped up: another move might require I give up her furniture. But these thoughts I put away like the two boxes of napkin rings. Into a drawer, some- where in my mind.

A year ago November, I did face another move, and was not excited about packing *anything* in Aunt Vi's buffet. Reluctantly, I pulled open the top drawer. There they were: my sister's napkin rings. All that bling going to waste. I could not, I realized, pack them up one more time. Linda's gift could do so much better than hide in a drawer. Who knew, maybe someone else might really enjoy them. And so I boxed them up, along with old knitting nee- dles and doilies, and dropped them off at Goodwill. Everything else I put in storage, including Aunt Vi's dining room suite. I was now in limbo, betwixt and between real estate choices, complexity eclipsing simplicity.

A few weeks later, Christmas quickly approaching, I popped into Goodwill to browse and found myself wandering down one of the home décor aisles. The season awhirl full tilt, I felt a little down, depressed, a little disoriented. Glitz, glamor, gifts none could afford, canned music piped into the stores. When "I Saw Mommy Kissing Santa Claus" came on for the umpteenth time, I plotted my escape. This aisle, turn left, pass the cash registers . . . I zipped my coat as I went. What's this?

Out of the minutiae on a shelf, tucked into a box under a clear plastic top, shimmering gems and jewels adorning four brass rings caught my eye. Linda's box of napkin rings! The *emerald* set! It was like seeing old friends! I turned the box over. Four dollars. I should buy them back! "No, no, no," I told myself firmly.

Someone else will enjoy them more. Briefly, I wondered about the other set and where it might be in all the minutiae, but forced myself to keep going—and stopped in my tracks.

A little girl, all of six, at the other end of the aisle had found them, the ruby set. A sprinkle of freckles on her nose, short pig-tails poking out of a scruffy pink hat, her face held such longing. The mother, clearly impoverished, had plaited her own dark hair in a single braid that snaked over a shoulder. I eased toward them, picked up a doodad, and eavesdropped.

"Oh, Mama," the child said softly, wonder in her voice. "If we could just buy these, our Christmas dinner would look *soooo* beautiful . . . Please?"

Her mother stooped down, admired the napkin rings for a second or two, then put them back. "Dear," she said, gently chucking her little girl's chin, bringing the child's eyes up to meet her own. "You're right, sweetie, they are lovely, but we don't need them. You see? We have you. *You* will make our Christmas dinner beautiful."

I could hardly breathe. What a wonderful woman! Turning her heartbreaking "no" into a gift of love. *Sweetie, you're all we need to make our dinner beautiful.* Then, what a ninny I am! This little girl is the person who will better enjoy the napkin rings! I watched her sigh in resignation, take her mother's hand, the two moving on. I backstepped to get the emerald set and hurried forward to retrieve the ruby. *Where had the mother and child gone?*

There they were! Halfway down, the next aisle over. I approached, the two boxes of my sister's napkin rings in hand. "Merry Christmas," I said to the little girl, bending down and handing her both, ruby and emerald. Her eyes went wide. She gaped. "They're yours," I assured her.

"Oh, Mama!" she breathed, unable to take her eyes off the bedazzling, gaudy rings. "*Two* boxes! See, these are green! Oh, please?"

"We can't," said Mama.

I handed the woman a ten-dollar bill and told her the story. "All these years sitting in a drawer," I said, wrapping it up, "until this year it struck me that someone else could really enjoy them. I think I found her. You know, I hardly ever come in here, today I did. I don't know why. Feeling a bit listless, at odds and ends. Nostalgic, I suppose, for the old simplicity. But then I spotted a set of my sister's napkin rings that I'd donated last month. Your daughter spotted the other set, I wonder . . ." I glanced at the girl, attention absorbed by turning the boxes to let the plastic gems catch the light, suddenly no longer gaudy but luxuriously wondrous in her eyes. "Is this not," I asked her mother, "a small Christmas miracle?"

Tears rimmed the young mother's eyes.

"Take them," I urged. "It's Christmas. Goodwill, glad tidings, and all that."

Goodwill and glad tidings. Betwixt and between though I was, and a little lonely for the simplicity and sincerity of Christmas past, I felt the spark of rebirth. Gifts once loved can be loved again. And Aunt Vi's dining room suite, in storage with everything else, could wait. If it came to pass that my downsizing might force me to leave it behind, Aunt Vi—ever-present and not going away—will ever remain in memory, sacrosanct. And now this new memory to hold, Christmas napkin rings transformed, gaudy to splendiferous beauty, by the wonder of a child.

I left Goodwill full of my own wonder, alive to this not-so-small Christmas miracle—and in hope of more to come.

Staff Luncheon at the Consul's Residence, Peshawar
by Kenneth Meyer

Granger rested one hand on the rooftop parapet wall as he looked at the piece of doggerel he had written that morning. It was already over one hundred degrees Fahrenheit on the consulate roof, but he wore a floppy hat and sunglasses, so what was there to complain about? He stood listening to one of the cooling units. It was almost lunchtime.

At a small post like this one, there were no backup units and everything had to work. If the unit humming next to him crapped-out, all the comms gear would fry, and who would be blamed for that? Support Officer Granger. But the unit whirred efficiently.

Of course, he was no specialist on cooling or air conditioning, but in this small post with relief far away (except via cable—that was relief in words only, usually exhortations), everyone had to try and do everything, or anything.

These were his words on the paper:

Barricaded compound at twilight
Frontier scouts under the trees
Concrete barriers and your two eyes on the roof

You check out a vehicle passing by
Two men walk down the street—they're okay
In the daytime the mountains look singed
But now they're only dark outlines
The private guards perform their sunset prayers
And you perform a private prayer

He thought but didn't write: *To get out of here in one piece.* For some reason the anecdote about the army sergeant in World War I came to mind: someone blows the whistle and shouts, "Over the top!" None of the soldiers move. The sergeant shouts, "What's the matter? You apes wanna live forever?" Granger laughed and carefully folded the paper. He put it in his pocket. Perhaps he would tinker with it later.

He opened the trapdoor and descended the retractable step-ladder. He walked past the Communications door, which sported one of his favorite plaques in the whole consulate. It said: *Will Close for Buzkashi.* Beneath the cautionary note was a photo of two horsemen wrestling over a goat-head on an unidentified muddy field. Buzkashi was the equestrian game played by two teams of five-to-seven riders each, during which a rider leaned over, grabbed the goat-head, and rode downfield to score a goal by galloping between two posts. Carson, the communications officer, had gone with the consul to at least one such local match. And who could forbid him to do so? Whereas in a larger post there would have been four to six communicators, here there was only Carson. He was his own boss. In the far-flung posts there was a kind of autonomy—or freedom?

In the stairwell, the consul's secretary, Vicky, accosted him, *sotto voce:* "Is something going on between Jennifer and Blake?"

When Granger knew her in Tunisia, Vicky Adpil was single, but then he went off to one of the Foreign Service schools and didn't see her for two years. Now, she was here in Pakistan. It was a truism that if you hung around government service long enough and kept going overseas, you would meet the same people, again and again. In the Middle Eastern posts, the Indiana Jones types all knew each other, and in the China theater, owing to the length it took to get anywhere with that language, as well as other factors, those people were almost like a dedicated priesthood—one that included women—and they all knew each other. The habitues of those two regions were like members of big families.

When he met Vicky the second time, in Pakistan, she told him in the interim she had gotten married and divorced.

"How is that possible?" protested Granger. "It's only been two years . . ."

"That guy was crazy," declared his colleague. "I made a mistake."

Thus, it was time for another overseas tour. Foreign service logic.

But back to Jennifer and Blake, yes, there was something going on. One of the problems at these small facilities was that you knew more than you ever wanted to about your colleagues: who was sleeping with whom, who was a drunk, who was being punished by being sent here (although of course there were no such things as punitive assignments), who was about to be pulled out for having a nervous breakdown, and so forth.

"I couldn't say," said Granger primly. A diplomatic answer. From Granger's point of view, the challenge during such assignments was not to find out about colleagues' personal lives, but rather trying to hold such information at arm's length. Though a bachelor, Granger's entanglements were usually "outside." He had met several girlfriends at sessions of the British "Hash House

Harriers," a running club which had branches all over the world. His recent flame had been a French worker at one of the NGOs working in Afghanistan.

"I'm heading for lunch."

Vicky was clearly not satisfied with his response, but she nodded. "Me too. I just hope it isn't that red chicken again."

She referred to *tandoori murgh,* a chicken marinated in a sauce with cayenne and other ingredients, left to sit overnight, and then usually baked. A Granger favorite.

"Vicky, that dish was enjoyed by the Mughal emperors."

"Let them have it then. I'm for the beef *pilau.*"

They crossed the courtyard and entered the consul's residence, which was undergoing one of its many makeovers. At various times, the two-story building had served as residence-cum-office, then all the staff used it as an office building, but now it was back to being the residence for the current consul, Dr. Svenson, and his wife. Why couldn't people make up their minds?

All the U.S. staff in Peshawar was invited to lunch today, a regular occurrence at this post, which only had twenty Americans, including spouses. At least twice a week the whole group was there: the visa officer, communicator, political officer, economic officer (sometimes those two posts were filled by the same person), aid officer, two Drug Enforcement Agency officers, and so on, and spouses. Local curries would be variously endured or praised—and usually the same people complained or were delighted. Of the consulate lineup, Dr. Svenson was the area expert. The teams at such posts were usually divided between former military personnel (after all, who was better at surviving "rough" locations?), specialists, and a few scholarly types or people with an interest in the region. Granger was in the last group. He had even studied the local language, Pashtu, which he massacred on a daily basis speaking with the consulate help and guards at the front gate.

Support Officer Granger washed his hands in the hallway bathroom and entered the dining room, which contained a table that would seat sixteen. The food was served buffet-style.

Granger saw his old colleague, Dean, from the Baghdad days. Here, Dean was the administrative officer. He had bought Granger's used Datsun 280Z when he departed the Iraqi capital, and you had to stand by a man like that. That automobile might have been the only one of its kind in Baghdad. Granger thought it probably was. Although the thing was falling apart, you could get it up to a hundred and fifteen miles per hour in the evening on the unfinished Baghdad belt road. Who was going to be on the road to complain about you? Nobody.

Those were the good old days.

Dean's wife Liza—another party averse to *tandoori murgh*—was also at the table. Dean and Liza seemed to be having a lot of angry words lately, but he didn't need to know about that. You would think that a woman who hardly blinked at an explosion outside her house (something about a motorcyclist and contraband goods) would be able to keep marching through anything, but then, what was that quote about marriages being like icebergs? You only saw the one-tenth above the water. There were a lot of divorces in the diplomatic corps.

Granger, now forty-three, had never been married. He knew nothing about matrimony.

Dean, the erstwhile owner of the Datsun 280Z—he must have gotten rid of that thing, since he didn't bring it to Pakistan—was shoveling some *pilau*, rice and lamb, onto his plate. Since Dr. Svenson and his Swedish wife were away for the week, Dean was the acting principal officer—the acting chief of the consulate.

Next to Dean was Sprague, the security officer, in this location a person with endless worries, such as phoned-in threats, hostile local press coverage, the occasional scandal or indiscretion among the staff, and so on. Granger's usual comment to Sprague was, "I want to decrease the number of your cares, not add to them." He thought that so far he had been mostly successful in not adding to Sprague's burden. Unfortunately at this luncheon, Sprague had barely filled his plastic plate with *pilau* and some stuffed peppers when a local guard came in and whispered something in his ear. Sprague set down the plate and rushed out.

Granger didn't hear any cars crashing (which you did sometimes) or gunfire, so there was no emergency. He continued around the table helping himself to some of the *pilau*.

Emmy was the wife of one of the political officers. Although not a fan of Pakistan, she was usually cheery. She now looked up at Dean. "The guards said I should mention to you, Dean, that one of our guards shot someone and ran away."

The acting principal officer was picking up a piece of cake. The hand holding the plate trembled, but only slightly, and Granger would have expected no less of a colleague who had served in Baghdad. After all, in the latter assignment, missiles were hitting the city and a war was down the road. What was one measly shooting by a guard? But Dean was losing his hair, and lunchtime revelations like this were one reason why. "Oh?"

"Yes, he ran off into the tribal areas until things cooled down, but we wouldn't mind having him back when he can return. He's a good guy."

"He had a reason for shooting the person," Granger contributed encouragingly. Actually, he knew nothing about the incident.

"Of course he did. And the other person is in the hospital. He isn't dead," continued Emmy.

"Let's back up a little bit," Dean said gently. "He shot someone, but not while on duty."

The meaning here being: the consulate guards carried weapons, but the guards at your residence, usually only one person per shift, didn't.

"Of course not! He shot someone while off-duty—"

"And you knew something must have happened because he failed to come to work—"

"Yes," continued Emmy. "He shot the person and then ran off into the tribal areas to hide. Not that our guard was from the tribal areas. He just went there. The guards sent a replacement over; they're very considerate. And one of the guards explained— by making a pistol with his hand and 'firing' into the air—that our guard had shot someone. The neighbors suggested that we go off to the hospital and pay off the injured person, but I don't think we should do that."

"Good God, no," responded Dean. "You don't even know what it was about. If you start giving the injured party money, his family might come back and sue the consulate or something."

"And we shouldn't get in the middle of this," Granger suggested. *We don't even know what "this" is.*

"I'm not so sure we'd want to take the guard back even if it all does settle down," Dean said thoughtfully. "What if the tribe of the other person gets angry and some of the members start shooting up your place, looking for the guard?"

Several people around the table nodded.

"It's your safety we have to think about."

Emmy still felt she needed to explain: "Like I said, he's not from the tribal areas. He just went there because it's lawless."

The consulate was in the federally administered areas, but to the west were the "tribal areas" only loosely regulated by the central government. Granger had been doing quite a bit of reading up on all this, and even visited a few locales in the tribal zones. But he was no expert on the areas to the west. "You know, Emmy, I think members of the Afridi tribe would be very hurt if they heard you talking like that. Let's not say their area is *lawless*. Maybe we should just say they have their own traditional codes of what can be done and what can't be done."

"Put it *your* way, if you like," Emmy retorted. The tone of her voice was combative, but Granger knew they were actually the best of pals. "Anyway, we're willing to have him back."

Dean was moving to one of the seats along the wall. "We'll look into it. We have to be careful in such situations. After all, we're staying here. We're not going anywhere." The acting principal officer's tone suggested he wished he was going somewhere.

Granger sat down next to Blake, who was the public affairs and public diplomacy officer. Said colleague was playing with some *pilau*. "Granger, aren't you the writer?"

"Most editors say no," he admitted.

"One of our translators read your story about the police stopping the van downtown."

That was a fictional piece about someone speeding through a police check and the local gendarmes giving chase. Everyone winds up in the bazaar in the old town. The streets are so narrow the escaping van has to stop, and the driver gets out and starts running. The policeman chases the man but doesn't catch him. In the end the policeman is lying on the ground by the wreckage of a display he crashed into.

"My guy wants to translate the piece into Pashtu and publish it in the magazine *Sahaar*. Have you heard of *Sahaar*? I have to warn you it probably only has a circulation of about three hundred."

"That's three hundred more readers than I have now. Tell him, sure, it would be great if they use it."

"I'll do that."

Two colleagues were still discussing the business of the guard shooting someone, but Granger had had enough of that topic. At this post, with tribal feuds going on nearby, war in Afghanistan, and hostiles threatening the consulate on a monthly basis, the bar was set high for "threatening event." Guards doing something and running off didn't count as hair-raising. Unless a missile came flying in through the administration building window, all was "normal." Granger thought, *what a crew!* They had a certain *esprit de corps.* Most of them shared a set of psychological traits; they were unrufflable, pragmatic, focused, irrationally optimistic.

"We're standing by the *tandoori murgh!*" someone said.

Several colleagues laughed, some nervously, most in genuine amusement.

"We're not leaving," Granger intoned.

"No, we're not," Dean affirmed.

Outside, Granger pulled the paper out of his pocket, spread it out on the residence wall, and regarded the line:

And you perform a private prayer

He added:

A prayer for a night of crickets, cock-a-doodle-doo, and dripping water

Granger believed he was halfway through a day well-executed.

Radio Baseball
by Betty Ruddy

The late 1950s and early 1960s were a peaceful time for a young girl to grow up on ten acres outside a small town in the Midwest. Without a childhood filled with hours to spare and few worldly distractions, would I have discovered baseball on the radio, would I have become a lifelong baseball fan?

I didn't come to appreciate the Great American Pastime in the way my brothers or other boys did. I never played organized ball or collected trading cards from bubble gum packages. It was the slow-paced cadence of the radio game that pulled me in. The major league broadcasts were just a background buzz of voices when I was seven, but by the time I was ten, they had crept into my consciousness. They were the teacher I didn't know I had.

Of course, I always knew what baseball was. I played a version of it myself. Not long after my family took up residence in the former farmhouse on those ten acres—when my brother Chuck was six and I was eight—our father configured a ball diamond in the southwest corner of the property, up against the wooded fringe of the pond. It had a backstop of chicken wire and boards, a raised mound and bases. It was like playing in a shallow bowl.

When we had a first baseman, he stood partway up our shortest, steepest sledding slope.

But we rarely had a first baseman. In fact, we rarely had more than four or five boys from the neighborhood who joined us, and often, Chuck and I played alone—squinting at the dirty ball in the failing spring light, hoping to squeeze in one more round of our private version of flies and grounders or trying to move the last invisible runner home from third before dark.

When, at last, we left the smell of grass and dirt behind and made our way inside for dinner, the sonorous voice of the Detroit Tiger broadcaster, Ernie Harwell, was frequently rolling out of the radio on the kitchen counter. In many ways, he described a game quite different from the one we had just played. Our contests were childish creations, designed to fit the terrain, our mood, and the rules we settled on that day. How many bases do you take when the ball reaches the barn? How many outs should each inning have? If someone had to go home to dinner, we changed the scheme. We didn't pretend to be Al Kaline or Mickey Mantle. Each thing we did was for ourselves; it was our personal adventure.

Big league baseball, on the other hand, was a century-old contest played by grown men in front of large crowds. The games followed unvarying dicta that were precisely enforced. The player's skills were awe-inspiring. The manager moved players on and off the field with a grand scheme in mind. Professional baseball was like a complicated board game or puzzle. I loved puzzles and games, so I loved major league baseball, and the radio provided my instruction.

I was often too busy playing to listen to day games. But sometimes hot, humid afternoons without air conditioning left energy for little else. There was the summer my mother painted the five hundred feet of white fence along the road. If bored enough, I would squat next to her for an hour, now and then dipping paint the consistency of melted marshmallows out of the bucket, and baseball chirped as natural as the sound of crickets from my mother's radio sitting in the grass.

I also liked the sound of Harwell's voice on my blue plastic portable as I lay in bed at night. I preferred his voice to popular songs about true love and heartbreak, stories about things that I troubled over enough during the day—boys, being pretty, growing up. Baseball had a consistency and remoteness that was soothing.

When Chuck and I stayed for a week with grandparents in the city, we biked with our mitts and a ball to the city park, because a house now stood on the corner sandlot where our father had played when he was our age. The visit also meant time with my city girlfriends. They rarely picked up a bat or ball, but we were all enamored of Tiger players. Sure, we followed Fabian and Frankie Avalon and occasionally splurged on celebrity magazines. But the radio was free. My favorite Tiger was "Stormin'" Norman Cash, Tiger first baseman from 1960 to 1974. Perhaps I judged him good-looking. Or maybe I appreciated his longevity or statistics. All I remember is that being a young fan required having a favorite player.

I also followed Charlie "Paw Paw" Maxwell (nicknamed for his Michigan hometown), because Harwell said he had a penchant for hitting home runs on Sundays. In my mind's eye, I saw him fresh from church, stepping up to bat knowing in his heart he had a long ball due that day. How could that be, I wondered? What magic spoke to a player at the plate on one particular day of the week?

And what magic propelled the New York Yankees to the top of the American League eleven of the thirteen seasons from 1952 to 1964, my formative baseball years? I developed a dislike for the men in pinstripes, an affliction frequently found in fans who grew up near American League cities in those pre-divisional days. It seemed so unfair that other teams never had a shot at the pennant.

But during the regular season, I continued to absorb the nuances of the game. From Harwell's deep tones, I learned that a leadoff hitter reaching base—no matter how—is a thing of value, and "Walking" Eddie Yost knew how to draw a walk. He had a career high of 151 walks in 1956, tied with Barry Bonds at ninth place, and his career total (1,614) ranks eleventh in the Majors all-time. Baseball, I realized, was not a game for those who want a quick fix. Steadfastness over time—through pitches, innings, games, even years—carried the most weight, for both player and fan. Like most such fans, I like to know the numbers.

As an adult, I moved to Seattle. Even after the city obtained a Major League team, I continued to be a Tiger fan, rooting them to a World Series win in 1984. Eventually, though, I missed daily baseball broadcasts, and if I wanted to listen, it had to be a Seattle Mariners game. On spring and summer afternoons you could find me planting zucchini or in mortal combat with ivy vines, the radio sitting in the wheelbarrow like an obedient lapdog. The ninth inning came too quickly, and I longed for the days of frequent double-headers. In the evening, as in the home where I grew up, the game was always on in the background as we ate dinner and cleaned up after. Dave Niehaus provided my baseball lessons now, as the family rooted for Ken Griffey Jr. to hit yet another home run or the Mariners to finally break the .500 mark. The Mariner's first playoff series win in 1995 and tie of the all-time season-win total only stoked the flames of my enthusiasm. The 2022 return to the playoffs after eleven years was a joy; Rick Rizzs' voice now guided me through the exploits of J.P. Crawford and Cal Raleigh.

My husband referred to me as the "real fan" in the family, and his coworkers' wives asked me to explain the game. "Where did you learn so much about baseball?" they wanted to know. "How many games do you *go* to?" It's the radio game, I tried to tell them. But if you didn't spend hours listening as Harwell described doubles hit in the gap and managers arguing with umpires, if you didn't schedule your spring outdoor cleanup to coincide with spring training broadcasts, how could I convey the way baseball wove its way into the fabric of my life. The women appeared to respect my interest, but I suspect they wondered why I bothered.

But there were many women who bothered—my Aunt Louise, for one. In the 1950s, she and a "neighbor lady" would take the bus and then a streetcar from the suburbs to Tiger Stadium at the corner of Michigan and Trumbull. More than once, family lore has it, she would lean over to a fan sitting nearby to correct some fact he had asserted about the team or the rules of the game. I can still see her standing in her spotless kitchen listening to the game on her beige radio as she made me a tomato sandwich for lunch.

I'm sure she would agree that baseball is so much more than autographs, home runs, or even the performances of the individual players. The game itself is the real Major League star, and the game on the radio is no pale substitute for the real thing. While the ballpark has its own noisy, smelly charms, the radio game is sharp and clear and lively. It is the real game without skipping the dishwashing or giving up gardening.

I don't garden any longer. I'm reading more and working with old books, so my mind is less free for me to do something with my hands while at the same time having one ear on a radio game. Sometimes, I even watch a game on television. But TV announcers don't have to provide vividly detailed descriptions of what's happening on the field. They don't lift my heart outside myself as do radio announcers—not as good as Vin Scully or Dave Niehaus but good enough—when they describe the smell of the grass, the dryness of the air, the crack of the bat, a ball arcing high in the air, or a runner heading for a close play at the plate.

I can imagine a time when I am as old as Aunt Louise during her last few baseball seasons, when the company provided by baseball will be most welcome. The radio game will feel like an old friend who has come to call, an old friend who always shows up when she says she will. The rules of the game will be the same (mostly, at least, despite rule changes like the pitch clock). Close plays will be argued and the manager's strategies second-guessed. The rituals surrounding the broadcast will be as comfortingly familiar as they are annoyingly full of clichés; the pre-game show will feature a "manager's corner," and a player on the post-game show will say: it's the win that counts, not what I did today.

I'll know who is pitching and what the score is. As a batter steps to the plate, as a pitcher walks off the mound to make way for a reliever, as the game ebbs and flows, the voices coming through my radio will carry both the excitement of another game and the measure of the game itself. And maybe the Mariners will be playing the Tigers in Detroit, the broadcasters will become nostalgic, and Ernie Harwell's voice will be played as tribute. I will recognize it the moment I hear it.

Spanish Beach Vacation
by Michaela von Schweinitz

We lost everything in Barcelona. Wolf's Beetle with our luggage inside and my family's borrowed camping gear tied to the roof. All stolen at the beginning of our three-week vacation, the day we arrived in Spain. The thieves had plenty of time while we were having pizza and sangria in a restaurant nearby. The only things we have left are the clothes on our backs and the money in our pockets.

Brigitte mourns the loss of her disco outfits and wants to go home to Germany. Wolf hopes to get his car back, and so we're staying. I don't know what makes me sadder, the loss of my clothes or the loss of the tent I'm expected to eventually bring back to my parents in perfect condition.

After two nights staying at a hotel, I'm running out of money. Of the three of us, I'm the one still in school. Camping was the only way I could afford this vacation, and the gear was my contribution to our trip. As luck would have it, the police find the Beetle, cleaned-out but not damaged. Tent or no tent, with Wolf's help, I convince Brigitte to keep going south. "We don't have fancy clothes, but we can still dance."

I met Brigitte and Wolf a few weeks ago at my favorite club, after I had ended a two-year relationship and lost all of our mutual friends in the process. Brigitte approached me in her skinny jeans to put her purse next to me while she danced. Then, I noticed Wolf's shock of blond hair. Tall and thin, he leaned against a wall with a drink dangling in his hand as he watched Brigitte. When he lifted his head to take a sip, his blue eyes lit up. Later that night, I found out Brigitte and Wolf had grown up together. They were a couple of years older than me, and right away, I longed to be a part of their easygoing friendship.

A few weeks later, we set out for Spain. At first, my parents worried about me going on this journey—they thought I was immature for my age. But I convinced them that my companions were decent, responsible people and so they gave me not only their camping gear, but lots of advice and maps. My new friends had never been out of Germany. But I had. I would be the navigator.

Now, we are driving in silence on the Autopista de la Mediterránia—the freeway along the coast. Sunburned cattle ranges rise and fall like swells in the ocean. Now and then, the silhouette of a big, black bull stands above the golden, grassy ridge. No livestock grazes in the shadow of these giants. What are these cutouts, leaning against scaffolding, advertising? Bullfights? Steak houses?

Desperate to lift the mood, I say, "Look, a bullboard."

Wolf focuses on the road, so I turn around to get Brigitte's reaction. She's asleep.

Each time the coastline dips, the dark blue of the sea appears below the bright sky. I wish we would get off this freeway already. I check the map I kept safe in my purse. I want to go swimming and would take any dirt road to get to the beach. But my friends want to go further south, far away from Barcelona. I'm about to crawl out of my skin when Wolf points at a sign on the side of the road. "Let's check it out. My friends told me about the beaches of Cap Calp."

Beaches. That's all I need to hear. We take the exit and soon see the mountainous rock of Cap Calp that gives the region its name jutting out from the coastline. We hit an intersection. A sign points left to the *Playas de Cap Calp* six kilometers north. With the beach so close, I am ready to dive into the ocean. Wolf points in the other direction. "Benidorm."

I never heard of the place and it's not on my map. "Funny name," I say and wait for him to turn left.

"That's where my friends camped." Wolf starts to turn right. "It's only twelve kilometers. Let's go there."

"But I want to go swimming, and we're so close to the beach." I turn to Brigitte for support. She's just waking up and offers no help.

Wolf is determined. "They stayed at a cheap campsite. Let's see if we can find it."

Twenty minutes later, we arrive in Benidorm. I hope for a refreshing shower, but a sign reads *completamente reservado*. The campground is full. Cars can't enter without someone opening the gate. My friends are at a loss, but I am not giving up now. "Look, they don't stop pedestrians. There isn't even a fence. We could enter anywhere we like." Convinced, Wolf parks at the small mercado across the street.

To justify our parking spot, we go inside to buy some food. A German family roams the aisles, kids trailing behind with ice cream and beach balls. Brigitte grabs a bottle of ice-cold Coke and some crackers. Wolf picks up a big bag of chips and a couple of candy bars. I pay for a loaf of bread and a bottle of water, and leave to wait for my friends outside. I wonder how long I will be able to keep up with them.

With the camping gear and all but one of the maps gone, I feel way off course and uncertain of my position with Brigitte and Wolf. Maybe it would be better to cut our trip short and return home. I shake the thought out of my head and feel the perm, the one I got for my boring, blond strands after admiring Brigitte's long, brown curls. I am in Spain. The sun is shining, and I will go swimming with my friends.

Grocery bags in hand, we enter the campground. Dressed in jeans and T-shirts, we look like any other campers returning from shopping. Nobody stops us. We walk on dirt compressed into a hard crust through a maze of dust-caked tents. No trees offer shade. It's quiet—most people are probably at the beach.

We search for the facilities. They aren't hard to find. The pictograms for women and men are the only color on the bare concrete. Wolf nods toward the men's side. "I won't take long but you girls take your time. I will scout the place and see if I know anyone. I'll meet you here."

I follow Brigitte into the women's side and I slap my forehead. "We forgot to buy toiletries."

Brigitte hesitates and I almost bump into her. "We don't have towels, either."

I don't care. Inside the floors are wet, like they were recently hosed down, and the showers are clean. A new bar of white soap beacons from a washbasin. I take it.

We have the showers to ourselves and choose two stalls facing each other. I enjoy the water on my body. For a moment, I stop worrying about where we will sleep tonight. When Brigitte asks for the soap, I'm glad I can share something with her. I have no problem stepping out naked to hand her the bar.

Refreshed, we wait for Wolf outside on a bench. We don't wait long. His smile is visible from afar. His tussled hair is still wet from the shower. He can't contain his excitement. "I met a guy who will let us stay in his tent."

Brigitte looks surprised. "What guy?" she says, not getting up from the bench.

Wolf's voice betrays his pride about his discovery. "He's a photographer from Germany. His name is Thomas."

"Why would he let us sleep in his tent?" I follow Brigitte's example and stay put.

"He sleeps in his camper and has a spare tent. He'll let us stay on his site." Wolf steps from one foot to the other. "Come on. I'll show you."

We follow Wolf through the labyrinth of tents into an area where there are more RVs. I'm amazed by the luxury on display— stoves, refrigerators, even TV sets. I feel the sting of envy.

Wolf points at an orange igloo tent. "Look, there it is."

My heart sinks. The thin, nylon fabric is almost see-through. A far cry from my father's sturdy canvas tent. Wolf knocks at the door of a midsized camper.

A bare-chested man with short, dark hair opens the upper half of a Dutch door.

Wolf gestures towards the orange blob. "I see you put the tent up already."

"Yeah. I've never pitched it before and wanted to see what it looks like."

"That's nice of you to let us stay in your tent," I say. "Can I have a look?"

"Go ahead. There's no key."

I open the zipper, hoping to find it to be larger than it looks from the outside. I can't picture the three of us sleeping in here. We can't even stand upright, like we would have in my father's tent.

Brigitte takes a brief look over my shoulder. "What will we sleep on?"

We were supposed to sleep on my family's comfortable blue air mattresses. All gone, along with the tent, the lantern, the hammock, and the cooking gear. I had also planned to use the mattresses to float on the water—the main attraction for fun at the beach, at least in my mind. Now I had no chance to share that fun with my friends.

Thomas pulls me out of my brooding. "Listen, I haven't had my siesta yet. I have two sleeping bags somewhere. Come back in an hour or two. Hasta luego." He closes the camper door.

Brigitte raises an eyebrow. "Two sleeping bags?"

"It's warm. I don't need anything." Wolf wants to move on. "Let's go check out the beaches of Cap Calp."

I zip up the empty tent so mosquitos stay out. At least there is nothing to steal here.

We take the coastal route through the beach communities. Bikini-clad tourists are crossing the streets, disregarding traffic lights. Some have towels draped over their shoulders. Others have little children in tow, ice cream dripping from their fingers.

The massive rock of Cap Calp comes into view. Something else becomes visible the closer we get—high-rises encroach on the idyllic bay. They seem misplaced, as if a giant forgot his building blocks at the beach.

I buy the least kitschy beach towel with a palm tree on it at a shop that sells everything from fruits to fiction. Brigitte checks out the book covers. "I had packed two books. Now I don't have anything to read at the beach."

I didn't know she was a reader. We have something in common, other than dancing. "What books did you bring to read?"

"I don't know. I just grabbed something from the shelf while waiting at the cashier."

I can't afford to buy anything other than food and water. But even if I had the money, I would never buy a book at the supermarket. I bury myself in books for hours before I decide which one to buy at my local bookstore. Brigitte picks up a thick tome of light reading. "How do you know you will like it?"

She shrugs her shoulders. "I like the cover."

Curious, I tilt my head to read the title. She holds it up to me. "Do you want it? I'll get another."

"No. Thanks."

"You all done here?" Wolf approaches us with a towel in psychedelic colors over his shoulder. He fixes his unruly hair with a comb he purchased. "Let's get to the beach before the sun is gone." He plucks a sombrero from a rotating rack and puts it on. He bends to check his image in the small mirror at the top of the display. It's one of those straw-braided hats I've seen in the streets. He turns and puts it on my head. "Let's go."

"Looks good on you," Brigitte says. "You should get it."

I laugh and put it back. "It's too big for me."

We cross the street and find a sunny spot on the crowded beach between umbrellas and other beach gear. I gaze at the blue sea and can't sit. "Who wants to go swimming?"

"I just showered." Brigitte grabs her book.

"I want to go swimming."

"Go ahead. I'll watch your towel."

Wolf takes his jeans off and I hope at least he will join me. His strong legs look good in his blue trunks. I'm glad I put my bikini on earlier and undress. Wolf is ahead of me, walking toward the water.

This late in the day it's not so hot anymore, and I slow down to let my feet sink deeper into the fine sand. I enjoy the way it feels between my toes. I look up and see Wolf's slender body against the sun, his feet ankle-deep in the water. I run past him, splashing into the waves. I want him to follow me so we can frolic around.

The water is warmer than I expected. I swim in long strokes. My body stretches and moves without restriction. Wolf doesn't follow me. I'm a little taken aback, but soon enjoy having this moment to myself. I'm in my element. Swimming is like breathing. I reach a red buoy warning motorboats not to enter the little bay. From here, the high-rises at the shore are small compared to the towering rock.

I sense that I'm not alone anymore. A plastic tube travels through the water ahead of me. A snorkeler. His head emerges and he looks around as if lost.

He sees me, takes the snorkel out of his mouth and shouts in German, "This is amazing!" Enjoying the swim, I agree, but then he asks, "Have you seen this?" He bites on the mouthpiece and looks down with his goggles.

I'm not sure what to think of *this*. The tube moves in my direction but stops at an appropriate distance. He looks up. "You've got to see this."

"What do you mean?"

He takes his goggles off, dips his head underwater, comes up, and whips his brown hair back. He doesn't seem much older than me. "Here. Take these and have a look." He hands me the goggles and smiles.

I've never snorkeled before and I'm not sure about the mouthpiece. He must have read my mind. "I'm not sick. It's okay." He flushes the tube a couple of times while I fit the goggles to my face. Below me, a new landscape appears. Underwater sand dunes stretch out as far as I can see. They have ripples that remind me of the fine lines of sand the waves make each time they retreat from the shore.

I come up for air. "Wow, I've never seen the bottom of the ocean."

"Keep looking. Here, you have to bite down on it and close your lips around it."

I do as he says and almost swallow the saltwater that comes through the tube.

"You have to look down to get air."

With my face underwater, I breathe through the snorkel. It is strange at first, but soon I get used to it. I hear him ask, "Do you see them?"

Indeed, a bright yellow fish with a blue fin appears near me. Amazed by the contrasting colors, I follow it with my eyes until another fish crosses in front of me. This fish's red tail fans out like a long, thin veil. I've never seen any fish like it, not in the ocean, not on TV, and not in the little pet store in my hometown.

I am thrilled. I lift my head out of the water. "These fish are so beautiful and the water so clear." I had moved farther away than I'd intended, and swim back to return the equipment.

He shares my excitement. "You know what, keep snorkeling. I've seen enough. Here, take these too." He is wearing flippers. "These allow for the least movement so you won't disturb the fish." He hands me a flipper and I try to put it on my foot while treading water with the other. The flipper doesn't fit and I struggle to stay afloat. "You can adjust the strap to your size." I'm thankful he tightens the other one before he hands it to me.

"Where on the beach are you? I'll bring them back to you." I turn toward the shore. It's so far that I can't even see where Brigitte must be reading her book.

"Keep them. I'm flying home tonight."

I'm touched by his kindness. "Wow. Thanks."

"Enjoy." He waves goodbye and swims toward the shore.

I can't believe my luck. Our first day at the beach and already I've seen exotic fish in the most pristine water. Wolf has scored a place for us to sleep for free. Brigitte is watching over my towel. And now I have something new to share with my friends.

I snorkel until I don't see any more fish. I come up and marvel at my good fortune.

Show Them Love
by Lorinda Boyer

Shielding my eyes against the glare of the sun, I peer down Fourth Street, anxious for the festivities to begin. The Seattle Pride parade is heavily attended, attracting upwards of three hundred thousand people each year. Staking claim to a piece of sidewalk early is essential, but after two hours of waiting, I'm impatient. I bop from one foot to the other. Sandy's hand closes around mine. She pulls me into her, plants a kiss on my cheek.

"I adore you, wife!" she declares.

I giggle. "And I adore you, wife!" We wrap our arms around each other's waists.

Living in northwest Washington, and especially here in Seattle, we are afforded a level of acceptance more generous than other places. Still, there are pockets in surrounding areas of my hometown of Bellingham where I feel insecure. Places where I avoid holding Sandy's hand or kissing her, where I consciously try to blend. But here, today, surrounded by our people, our culture of love and acceptance, I'm a part of the majority for a change. I allow myself to relax.

From somewhere behind me a voice booms, "Homosexuals, turn from your wicked ways!" I turn to see a dozen middle-aged men gathered under a coffee shop eave on the corner. Formally attired in slacks and button-down shirts, they pump their fists in the air. Pits wet with perspiration, they wave their placards declaring all gays are doomed to hell. A short guy clutching his bible in one hand, erratically waving a sign in the other, yells, "Adam and Eve, not Adam and Steve." I roll my eyes. Such *godly* gentlemen. Clean-shaven, short haired, voices dripping with hatred. A blight against the otherwise colorful crowd. I ignore them.

On the opposite side of the street, a queen perches atop a platform flanked by gigantic amplifiers. Extravagantly festooned in glittery platform heels and a sequined, strapless, peacock-blue dress, she laughs into a cordless microphone. "Welcome, Seattle!" She pauses, grins, bats her enormous eyelashes while we all shout and clap. She holds her hand up for quiet. "Welcome Seattle to your fortieth Pride Parade celebration!" The spectators erupt in deafening applause.

The dykes on bikes, Seattle Pride's official leaders of the parade, throttle their motorcycle engines. Clad in leather, Lycra, and in some cases, nothing at all, they tear down the middle of the street. Sandy whistles and claps. I raise my hands up and attempt to catch pieces of multicolored confetti before it floats to the ground. Two individuals dressed in decorated military uniforms march side by side. One carries the American flag, the other the Pride flag. I lay my right hand over my heart as I wonder why uniting us can't be as simple as this.

A cherry-red convertible carrying the mayor of Seattle rolls down the street at the heels of Seattle's Rainbow City Marching Band. The band's members sway in choreographed motion to the music. Primary-colored balloons, rainbow flags, feathers, and copious amounts of glitter adorn dancers, singers, marchers, and those simply caught up in the thrill of it all. Fourth Street is transformed into an endless, most raucous, musical.

I've nearly forgotten the negative protesters until I hear, "Turn from your wickedness!" The words spew wet on my exposed shoulder; I turn around as the men from the corner push their way between my wife and me. Our clasped hands are forced apart. Terror triggers my fight-or-flight response and I freeze. Not careful where they step, whom they shove, or in whose ear they bellow, the men barge through the swarm of people lining the curb. My heart pounds in my chest as I search for Sandy, who has seemingly disappeared.

The roar of the crowd is louder than the band of demonstrators, but their commotion catches the attention of the drag queen in the peacock-blue dress. In one swift motion, she powers up the mic, presses it to her lips. "Uh-ohhhh!" she singsongs, "Seems we have some angry fellas." She tsks, clucks, shakes her head. Parade-goers maneuver about, craning their necks to locate the men she's referencing.

I spot Sandy's head pop up above the crowd, then she vanishes. I wiggle my way through the bodies, hopeful I'm headed in my wife's direction.

The men, undeterred by the queen's acknowledgement, continue to rant with greater intensity. "Being gay is not the way!" "God hates gays!" They've managed to wrestle their way onto the street, filling a lull in parade activity. Disjointed in their approach, the men veer off in opposite directions, bellowing over the top of one another. The effect is chaotic, unpredictable.

I hunch my shoulders, pull into myself as my feelings of vulnerability intensify. "Sandy!" My voice cracks. I'm close to tears when her face appears. I grab and squeeze tight to my wife's hand.

Sandy squares her shoulders, pulls me closer, her muscles tighten against me.

For decades, I struggled to come to terms with messages like those scrawled in sharpie across the men's cardboard signs. I searched to find my place in their world, in their beliefs, but there wasn't one. I'm learning that's okay; I've found my tribe. Even still, fear creeps in.

"You are safe," Sandy whispers in my ear.

Drawing strength from her reassurance, I stand a little taller.

"We love you even if you don't love us." The peacock queen's voice is unwavering. She tosses her silky, black hair over her shoulder, causing her rhinestone earrings to swing. In all honesty, I'm not feeling particularly loving, but I do my best to embrace the sentiment. "Come on y'all." She sweeps open her arms, her flawlessly sculpted bosom bobbing with the movement. "Let's show these boys some love!"

As if on cue, a float bursting with posh drag queens slows in front of the peacock queen. Garmented in gowns, miniskirts, and hot pants, with their faces close-shaved, as well as fully bearded and mustached, the drag queens leap from the flatbed. Without hesitation, they link arms like Rockettes and skip in unison toward the men. The peacock queen twirls on her heel, pushes a few buttons. Sister Sledge's "We are Family" blasts from the speakers. A collective cheer emerges from the crowd.

The men glance warily at one another as the queens shimmy up and thread arms with them. I half expect the men to retaliate, to use their signs as weapons. Instead, one by one, the men drop their posters to their sides, eventually discarding them altogether.

I scrutinize their faces. Squint my eyes to get the most accurate take on their expressions. For sure, not all the men are smiling, but neither do they look infuriated. Rather, they appear confused, a bit freaked out, quieted. I watch as the elaborately painted and coifed queens coax the stoic men forward. The men move in step with their new friends. I gaze in amazement as they amble down the street, arm in arm, none pulling away.

As they disappear into the sun, I turn to my wife. "Did that just happen?"

She nods, her mouth open, her eyes wide.

"And that, Seattle," the peacock queen pirouettes and throws her arms in the air, "is how we show LOVE!"

Once again, the masses yell, scream, whoop, and holler. My shoulders relax. I feel a glimmer of hope that love, in fact, can conquer hate.

William Carlos Williams Inspires Mick Jagger
by C.J. Prince

If Mick wakens
as the sun bursts
over treetops
everyone asleep

if with the ecstasy
of movement
calling,
he tiptoes barefoot

down the hall
to the north, the blinds amber drawn—
the mirror inviting nakedness
as the song erupts wild in his mind—

a little bit louder now,
he swirls his nightshirt overhead
his voice louder, louder, and now
dancing, gyrating, singing

wild with all his body
raging in abandonment
"I've been lonely for so long."
The grotesque and eloquent body

face, arms, shoulders,
buttocks, pelvis, wailing
to the song in his heads,
yearning for a stage.

Persephone & Brigit Whisper
by C.J. Prince

In the whine of winter
people still hide
from people—contagious
still—this pandemic.

Barren trees outlined
in moonlight—
at dawn the shoreline
lazes
with the glint of snow.

Lifeless, no path—
walking along misty memories
Oregon grape, cedar, yew,
forgotten in the rising fog.

Beneath the surface,
deeper than moles and earthworms,
a stirring,
as Brigit
stretches fingers sunward.

This heart-thumping spring
rises up—
hellebores bloom,
crocus, tulips,

hyacinth—dazed.
Persephone inhales.

No matter wars, torture,
pandemic madness,
the earth opens
her rested soul,
the profound change—
a miracle,
unclaimed.
Rooted spring.

Nothing is Guaranteed
by Martha Oliver-Smith

Since we left Wells, Nevada, where we spent the night, the sky has been unusually pallid, a relief from the continuous hard glare of the relentlessly blue, western dome. For most of the day the sun has been hardly noticeable, a frail disk. The disk has been growing larger, its pallor shifting to rose pink, then to shades of red, crimson, vermilion, scarlet. At three-thirty in the afternoon, the sun is disappearing—not setting, but smothering in smoke. On the radio we've heard that The Mosquito Fire has been burning for ten days on the western slope of the Sierra Nevada Mountain range. We are nowhere near the actual fire, but the smoke has been rolling in our direction as we head toward Reno, our destination for the day. As we get closer to the city, the sepia miasma swallows the sun's red brilliance.

My husband Stephen and I and our small dog, Mateo, are travelling across the country from Vermont to visit my children on the west coast. Stephen and I are good travelers together. We married late, in our fifties, after we'd each learned some hard lessons from failed marriages. Now we are old, in our seventies. We know it's a gamble to be driving so far at our age during a pandemic and climate doom. We're not ready to fly yet with

COVID-19 still a big risk, and we're still wary of going into crowded spaces where few people are wearing a mask. We pace ourselves, taking turns driving, not pushing too hard or too fast. Today we are heading for Reno where we'll spend the night, our last leg of this part of the trip before we reach San Francisco tomorrow where we'll stay for several days with my daughter.

As smoky air seeps in through a back window left open a tiny crack for Mateo, I grab my long scarf and wrap it lightly around my mouth and nose. It has served me well as protection from overzealous air conditioning and ravenous mosquitos who love to bite me. The light fabric is printed with stripes that are actually pencils in different shades of red, purple, pink, yellow, green, and blue, a design adapted from a photograph of the colored pencils discovered laid out on the desk of the architect Frank Lloyd Wright a few days after his death. Stephen bought it for me in the MOMA gift shop in New York a few years ago. On this trip through the September days of our long travels, it has been chilly enough at times that I've needed to keep the scarf on, in or out of the car. Now it serves me as an air filter and a security blanket.

Even as we drive through the thickening smoke, I am feeling nostalgic about seeing Reno, "The Biggest Little City." I went to graduate school at the University of Nevada on a teaching fellowship and lived in the city for seven years. During that time, I discovered that I loved teaching, that I was a teacher. I went on to a long career teaching high school and then community college courses until I retired a few years ago. I have a fantasy about making a quick visit to the university campus in the morning before we head to San Francisco. Everyone I knew back in the early '80s is gone, but I would like to see the nineteenth-century buildings and grand, old trees spaced around the quad, a separate universe poised at the top of Virginia Street, which leads directly into the downtown, twenty-four-hour casino world.

I haven't broached the idea of stopping to see the campus with Stephen yet—he is not impressed with Nevada, so far, and does not want to linger. Having no interest in gambling, he finds the garishness of the casinos depressing. When we passed through the small towns of Wendover at the Utah border and then Wells, we saw no centers or main streets, just strips, blocks of casinos, built with giant minarets, turrets, and domes the size of Turkey's Hagia Sophia, throbbing with lights and blinking signs advertising the paradise of roulette, poker, craps, free drinks, and all-you-can-eat breakfast buffets.

Traveling with a dog limits our choices of motels. Finding a pet-friendly place is one of the daily anxieties of the trip. This afternoon, as we're heading into the smokey unknown, my unease about finding a place to stay has already begun. I'm also remembering the strange motel we stayed in two nights ago in Douglas, Wyoming.

It was late, almost 7:00 p.m., as we drove into town. We spotted the innocuously named Douglas Inn about half a mile into the strip, a squat, sprawling, flat-roofed, bleached-brick building with an overgrown lawn full of prickly weeds and an almost empty parking lot—a sign there would be a vacancy. It was the kind of place that would likely host a dog for a reasonable fee. The rundown exterior had not prepared us for the front lobby, another universe altogether. We entered what appeared to be a Bollywood movie palace the size of a football field. Once through the creaky, revolving entrance door, we were greeted by a life-sized, stuffed Siberian tiger, regally reclining, the first and only being to greet guests as they dared to enter his sanctuary. A dismissive sniff from Mateo proved the tiger to be no threat to our safety.

Behind the tiger, an atrium soared several stories high over a large shrine with a shining, copper roof. Inside the shrine festooned with strings of bright orange lights, lush tropical plants hung from the ceiling. Several plaster lions, about the size of Mateo, stood frozen amid a jungle of plants in giant pots on a floor carpeted with white gravel. In back of the shrine, a series of arabesque arches hovered over an Olympic-sized pool full of turquoise water stretching all the way to the back of the building. In spite of the ubiquitous orange lighting, the place was dark and full of shadows. Blinking along the cavernous side walls, myriad video games throbbed and burbled in the darkness.

Not a soul appeared to be staying in the motel. The very polite manager at the front desk, the only apparent employee, sent us through several sets of metal doors opening into many long hallways until we found our ordinary and clean motel room. The manager gave us one of his business cards in case we needed something. The card, ornate with gold curlicues on a dark magenta background, had his name and cell number printed in white, "Mr. S. Singh."

On the back of the card was another curlicue and a cryptic message: "Nothing is Guaranteed." At the time, we laughed at the ominous words, but I wondered a bit anxiously what this might signify for us.

Now as we make our way in this miasma of smoke toward Reno, "Nothing is Guaranteed" echoes in my mind. We are within fifty miles of Reno when we stop in Fallon for gas and groceries. It's already hard to breathe the air here. The fire may be more than a hundred miles away, but the smoke is settling in quickly. We must get ourselves into town and find a place to stay. As we approach the city, Stephen drives while I try to locate familiar territory, street signs and place names. I used to know all the ways to enter Reno, but now I recognize nothing. The streets have transformed into swooping freeway entrances and exit ramps that didn't exist when I lived here.

Then I realize we are not in Reno at all, but in Sparks, Reno's sister city. I remember it as a funky little town, but nothing here is familiar, either. We might as well be driving blind, the air thick with smoke and the streets almost totally dark. I wonder why it's so dark—and where are all the lights, the blinking, blaring casino lights? The streetlights? The streetlights are not working.

We can't breathe with the windows open and we can't see with them shut. Our own headlights seem useless as oncoming cars blind us. We can't stop and we don't know where we are going. Stephen is swearing. Trying not to panic, I glimpse a small, neon sign still alive on our right—a motel—and what seems to be a driveway. I yell: "Motel, Motel, Super 8, Super 8!!" Stephen lurches into the almost invisible driveway, just missing the curb. We are at least off the suicidal road, but the parking lot looks full. We have to try. There's no going anywhere from here.

I stay in the car with the dog and make promises to the universe while Stephen goes into the motel lobby to see if there's still a room available. The Super 8 is a motel chain we jokingly call "The Supperate." The rooms often smell like meat loaf and cigarettes, even if they are supposedly nonsmoking. But they usually take dogs and are relatively cheap. A Super 8 has saved us more than once. But as the card lurking in my purse insists, "Nothing is Guaranteed." I remind myself that the wait is a good sign he hasn't been summarily dismissed. The stifling, smoky air is thick enough that I wrap my scarf loosely around my nose and mouth again. I contemplate our possible fate, or perhaps our luck, and take nothing for granted.

As it turns out, the universe relents and provides a room. We unload our clunky luggage—duffle bags, shopping bags of food, dog bed, and a small cooler—onto a rickety metal cart. I will find our room and unload the baggage while Stephen parks the car and walks the dog.

I push through the doors of the motel into a small, no-frills lobby mobbed with people pushing and shouting at each other. A man is arguing with the woman behind the desk—a muscular, blond woman with an air of authority, the only person handling the crowd. Others are milling around waiting to get in line to shout at her, but she's holding her ground.

Then I remember COVID, another thing to be afraid of. I didn't put on a mask. Nobody in the crowd is wearing one. I immediately imagine the invisible virus spraying from the mouths of the angry shouters. I'm trying to move the cart in the direction I think the elevator must be, but I'm stranded in the narrow space of the lobby between the front desk and a wall lined with slot machines and video games. People stream around me and my cart, passing me in both directions. A large man in a T-shirt that doesn't cover his gut, lumbers toward me, "Watch where yer goin', lady," he snarls.

Head down, I try to push the cart forward, but I can't move. I feel dizzy. I have escaped from the smoky air outside, but inside, the atmosphere feels thick and dense, and it's hot. Where am I? Who am I? What am I doing here? I seem to have fallen into a crack in the universe. I can't find a way out of this hellish place. I'm stuck.

"I like your scarf."

I look up to see a young girl standing in front of me, her eyes bright and brown, looking at me. She is tall, the same height as I am. Her pale face, framed by thick, dark hair, is about two feet away from mine. She is heavyset—a big girl. She looks about sixteen years old.

"Pencils," she says.

"Yes. Pencils." I agree.

"You're a teacher," the girl says.

Who is this person? I look at her face, wide cheek bones, brown eyes full of intelligence and humor. I've never met her, but I know this girl. If she had been a student in my classroom, she would have been someone I recognized as a kindred spirit. Not a teacher-pleasing student with A+ grades. Too much humor and no-bullshit in those eyes. We would have recognized each other. Do recognize each other.

"Yes, I'm a teacher. I mean, I was," I add, realizing that now I probably look like a lost old woman out of her depth. "I'm retired."

We smile, and for me, something has shifted, a click, a switch.

She turns toward a woman standing behind her, probably her mother. They are the same height and shape. I want to thank her but can only silently wish them well as they too are pushing their way through the crowd. I shove the cart forward, parting the restive line in front of the counter where the stern blond manager is laying down the law: "I told you—one at a time—get back to the end of the line, sir!" A few more steps and I can see the elevator, waiting to take me up three floors to our room. I remember that I was a teacher, something to hang onto in the moment. But what else am I, other than a confused old woman vulnerable to her fears, undone by smoke from the fire and the pressure of an angry crowd? The answer is still up in the air.

The next morning, the air outside is no better than the night before, barely breathable. There will be no visiting the UNR campus. We drive out of Sparks and Reno on I-80 up the mountain.

The air gradually clears as we climb. We stop at the Donner Pass rest area where the smoke has relinquished the sun back to a blue sky. The sun may be out, but it's chilly at the top of the pass. I put on a sweater and wrap my pencil scarf around my neck. Though the fabric is light, it warms me. We stop to read the memorial plaque to the doomed Donner Party. No guarantees for them, not for any of us. No one would bother to take chances otherwise.

I will not forget the girl who called out "Pencils" as I was lost, floundering in the hot, dense air among the crowd, the shouting, and the fear. She saw me—not the pathetic old woman possessing me, but the person I was, I am—a teacher, a person who knows a few things. I guess the universe sent her to remind me of that. I wonder what she is doing in her life, if she will find a rewarding way to direct that quick, perceptive gaze, and the impulse to connect as she makes her way through the world. I hope so. But then, nothing is guaranteed.

Biographies

Amanda Stubbert fuels her passion for storytelling with degrees in psychology and theater, and pulls stories from others as a writing coach, editor, producer, and book-launch specialist. She is currently developing a tragically funny coming-of-age-in-the-'80s memoir about finding balance between absentee men and unrealistic expectations.

Andrea Gabriel and **Janna Jacobson** are a writing-and-life duo who live in Chippewa Falls, Wisconsin, with more elderly, four-footed creatures than is necessary or advisable. *The Zoo* came about when the pair—deep in the miasma of the pandemic—teamed up for the NYC Midnight Short Story Competition.

Anneliese Kamola is an author and developmental editor living in Bellingham, Washington, on the unceded land of the Lummi and Nooksack people. She has studied storytelling for over twenty-five years via writing, theater, dance, and psychology. Her work focuses on intergenerational trauma, healing, and the messy work of being human.

Beth Kress grew up in the Midwest and raised her family in Camden, Maine. Her work has been published in her chapbook, *Taking Notes*, and in the *Snowy Egret*, *Spotlight*, *The Avalon Literary Review*, and *Dreamers*. Beth recently won The Willow Review Prize. She lives in Arlington, Massachusetts, with her husband.

Betty Ruddy lives in the Pacific Northwest where she pursues her love of books, swimming, and grandchildren. Her essays have appeared in *Fourth Genre, The Journal,* and *Brain, Child.* Two of her essays were named Notables by *Best American Essays.* She has an MFA from the Bennington Writing Seminars.

Brenda Wilbee has written ten books, her *Seattle Sweetbriar* series selling six hundred thousand copies. Currently, she is working on a memoir and directs the Tinsy Winsy Studio, where she works with small publishers and other writers to take their stories from concept to conclusion: editing, typesetting, illustrating, layout, cover, and upload.

Carla Shafer, Jack Straw Writer selected in 2023, has poems in *Whatcom Places II* and *I Sing the Salmon Home.* An S.C. Boynton winner, she has several chapbooks. She was host of the Chuckanut Sandstone Writers Theater Open Mic (1991) and published the 2021 anthology, *Solstice: Light and Dark of the Salish Sea.*

Carol McMillan is an award-winning writer whose work has been published in several anthologies and scientific journals. She is the author of *White Water, Red Walls*, chronicling her rafting trip through the Grand Canyon, and *Scriptless*, a memoir of San Francisco in the 1960s.

C.J. Prince, poet and artist, is published in many anthologies, including *Women Write from the Heart of the West, 56 Days of August, The Fondis Chronicles, Catching My Breath*, and poetry book, *Mother, May I?* Prince received the Distinguished Poet medal from Writers' International Network, Vancouver, British Columbia.

Cynthia Tuell taught writing—basic, ESL, freshman comp—for forty-plus years, most recently at the University of California, Riverside. She was widowed when her children were very young and thus she had her hands full. Still, her poems and short stories have been published in *Kayak, The Seattle Review*, and *Psychological Perspectives,* among others.

Dawn Quyle Landau lives in Bellingham, Washington. A Blog-Her/SheWrites 2015 "Voices of the Year" and Huffington Post 2015 "Must-Read Blogger," Dawn's work is featured in three Whatcom Writes anthologies; *Cascadia Weekly*; *Bucketlist Publications*; and *Tangerine Tango: Women Writers Share Slices of Life*, as well as *The Huffington Post* (2012-16). Read her work at talesfromthemotherland.me.

Debu Majumdar's novel, *Night Jasmine Tree*, won CIBA's Somerset award for literary fiction in 2018. His other works are *Sacred River: A Himalayan Journey* and four children's books, (the *Viku and the Elephant* series). His short story, "An Indian Picnic," was included in Red Wheelbarrow Writers' 2018 anthology.

Dr. Deidra Suwanee Dees' family descend from *Hotvlkvlke* (Wind Clan) and follow Muscogee stomp dance traditions. She wrote *Vision Lines: Native American Decolonizing Literature*. She is the Director/Tribal Archivist at the Poarch Band of Creek Indians. A Cornell and Harvard graduate, she teaches Native American studies at the University of South Alabama.

Drue BeDo is primarily a playwright and theater artist. However, from time to time, she picks up a rock and discovers a poem or a piece of prose beneath. Living in the PNW, Drue loves swimming in the Salish Sea and sitting in the company of old growth Cedars and Douglas Firs. Find her work at playscripts.com.

Edward Tiesse can see Mount Baker and the Canadian Cascades from his home. Nature's wonders and everyday life inspire and move him in profound ways. Edward's poetry has been published in *The Front Porch Review, The Sea Letter, Whatcom Writes* and *Proverse*.

Katie Fleischmann is an aspiring writer currently working on a memoir about her cancer diagnosis amidst the pandemic. Her daughter and reading stories have been her escape from life's hardships. When time allows, she steals moments to run, putter in the garden, or play in the kitchen.

Although a Whatcom County resident for nearly ten years, **Kenneth Meyer** spent most of his adult life overseas in government service, including in the China area, the Muslim world, and Europe. He has loved telling stories from an early age and participates in several writers' groups.

Linda Lambert merges the creativity of writing with the research components of library and information science (she likes to look things up!). She ghostwrites biographies, dabbles in fiction, explores family history in a bio-memoir, and crafts poems, her most recent appearing in the Rena Priest-edited *I Sing the Salmon Home.*

Linda Morrow spent most of her life in New England before moving to Bellingham ten years ago. She is grateful for the support of the Red Wheelbarrow writing community. Her memoir, *Heart of This Family: Lessons in Down Syndrome and Love* was published in 2020 by Sidekick Press. For more information, visit her website at lmorrow.com.

Lora Hein became the first woman hired as a backpacking ranger-naturalist in Yosemite in 1973. She earned an environmental studies degree from Sonoma State University before relocating to Washington State. After twenty-three years in parks, conservation, and public education, she writes to instill hope and fortitude into other women.

Lorinda Boyer is the author of *Straight Enough* (Sidekick Press, 2021). When she isn't writing, Lorinda works as a personal trainer and fitness instructor. She enjoys running, cycling, and coffee.

Marie Eaton, faculty emerita from Fairhaven College, recently found a new voice in poetry. She received the Sue C. Boynton Poetry Contest *Walk Award* in 2018 and 2021, published poems in *Whatcom Watch* and in Empty Bowl Press' 2021 collection, *Keep a Green Bough: Voices from the Heart of Cascadia.*

Martha Oliver-Smith is a retired college and secondary school literature and writing teacher and the author of a memoir, *Martha's Mandala* (Spuyten Duyvil Publishing, 2015). She lives in Albany, Vermont, where she is working on a second memoir, *Marnie's Voices*, about her mother, an author and eccentric parent.

Mary Camarillo's multi-award-winning debut novel, *The Lockhart Women* was published in June 2021. Her second novel "Those People Behind Us" is forthcoming in October 2023. Her poems and short fiction have appeared in publications such as *Sonora Review*, *Lunch Ticket*, and *The Ear*. She lives in Huntington Beach, California.

Maureen Kane is a mental health therapist in Bellingham, Washington. She is a winner of the 2022 Sue C. Boynton Poetry Award and her work has been featured in the *Writing Together, Rising Together People's Perspective Project*. Her book of poetry is called *The Phoenix Requires Ashes*.

Maurya Simon's poetry volume, *The Wilderness: New and Selected Poems*, received the Independent Booksellers Association's 2019 Gold Medal in Poetry. Her poems have been translated into Hebrew, French, Spanish, Greek, and Farsi. A University of California professor, she lives in the Angeles National Forest in California.

Michaela von Schweinitz is a German-American writer. An award-winning filmmaker and screenwriter, she lived in Los Angeles for fifteen years. When Michaela moved to New York City, a vibrant writing community welcomed her. Excerpts from her upcoming memoir, *Driving Lessons*, have been read on stage by Naked Angels NYC.

Born and raised in Beirut, Lebanon, **Nadia Boulos** immigrated to Bellingham, Washington, in 2001 where she now resides with her husband and two children. She graduated from Western Washington University with a bachelor's in business marketing, and she is currently a freelance web designer (Reset Web Design), social media manager for a publishing company (Elyssar Press), and web manager for the Whatcom Community College Foundation. Her poetry and short stories reflect her traumatizing experience as a child of war. She enjoys yoga, hiking, playing music, traveling, and spending time with her family.

Nancy Canyon is published in *I Sing the Salmon Home*, *Raven Chronicles*, *Water~Stone Review*, *Fourth Genre*, *Floating Bridge Review*, *Poetry Marathon*, *Labyrinth*, *Sue Boynton*, and more. Nancy holds an MFA in creative writing from Pacific Lutheran University. She teaches writing for Chuckanut Writers and coaches for The Narrative Project. Learn more at nancycanyon.com.

Now retired from a career in vascular surgery, **Roy Taylor** writes memoir when he isn't entertaining his grandchildren with mostly true stories of homesteading as a child in the Alaskan wilderness or surviving adolescence in the pine woods of central Louisiana. He published a story in a previous Red Wheelbarrow anthology.

Richard Little, a retired attorney, has published a novel, *City Haul*, and two collections of short stories, *Postcards from the Road* and *Jakey's Fork—A River's Journey*. His work has appeared in the *Santa Fe Writers Project*, the *Seattle Times*, and several anthologies. His website is ariversjourney.com.

Seán Thomas Dwyer is the author of *A Quest for Tears: Surviving Traumatic Brain Injury*, as well as fifteen published short stories. He is the host of the Village Books' monthly Open Mic, and he is now a "human book," titled Traumatic Brain Injury Survivor. He lives in Bellingham, Washington.

Sky Hedman loves to tell a good story. She shares her memoir and travelogues through her blog at skyandlynne.blogspot.com. The natural beauty and intelligent politics of Bellingham nurture Sky and her partner, Lynne, who migrated here in 2009. Their pandemic puppy takes them on daily walks in the park.

Sheila Dearden is a naturalist, writer, storyteller, voiceover artist, beekeeper, and lover of the outdoors living in the Pacific Northwest. She holds an MA in environmental education and a marine naturalist certification. Currently, she is working on a natural history memoir that explores the connection between landscape and the human heart.

Stephanie Sarver's writing has appeared in such publications as *Weber: The Contemporary West, Travelers Tales,* and *Literature Film Quarterly*. Her book of literary scholarship, *Uneven Land,* was published by the University of Nebraska Press. She lives in the Pacific Northwest, where she ponders the seasons and the paradoxes of human nature.

Susan Chase-Foster has lived in Mexico, and is currently polishing a collection of stories set in a fishing village where humidity can melt a brain, chachalacas never stop chattering, and her muses constantly take siestas. Her poems and stories appear in numerous anthologies. She is the author of *Xiexie Taipei.*

Victoria Doerper writes from her cottage near the shore of the Salish Sea. Her work appears in *Cirque; The Plum Tree Tavern; Bindweed; I Sing the Salmon Home;* and *Orion* magazine. Her book, *What If We All Bloomed? Poems of Nature, Love, and Aging,* was published in 2019.

Wendell Hawken (she/her) earned her MFA in poetry at Warren Wilson College, decades after her BA degree. Her publications include three chapbooks and five full collections. With two dogs, Hawken lives on a grass farm in the northern Shenandoah Valley where the first meaning of AI is Artificial Insemination.

Acknowledgments

Red Wheelbarrow Writers . . . you are the creators who come together monthly to share stories, create collaborative tales, and encourage novice and seasoned writers alike. Most importantly, you are the writers who made this book possible by your involvement in every step of the journey.

An enormous thank you goes to the following members for significant contribution to this volume:

Laura Kalpakian, Cami Ostman, and Susan Tive for the concept of our community.

Editors Laura Rink, Laura Kalpakian, Marian Exall, Randy Dills, Jean Waight, Joe Nolting, Susan Chase-Foster, and Victoria Doerper.

Lisa Dailey, publisher at Sidekick Press, Andrea Gabriel, cover design, and Dana Tye Rally, proofreading and editing, for their extraordinary publishing skills.

Thanks also to the many locations that have housed our monthly gatherings and for the technology of Zoom, which has allowed us to welcome new members from far and wide. Deepest heartfelt thanks to the wonderful team at Village Books, especially Paul Hanson, Kelly Evert, and Sarah Hutton, for ongoing support and cheerleading of writers in our greater community.